Start

Stop

NATIONAL GEOGRAPHIC KiDS

CODE THIS!

PUZZLES, GAMES, CHALLENGES, AND COMPUTER CODING CONCEPTS FOR THE PROBLEM-SOLVER IN YOU!

JENNIFER SZYMANSKI

NATIONAL GEOGRAPHIC
WASHINGTON, D.C.

CONTENTS

CHAPTER 1

CHAPTER 2

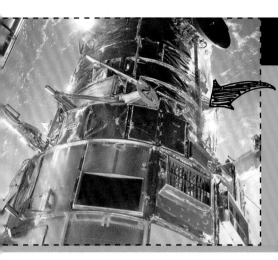

CHAPTER 3

CHAPTER 4

I'm a hair ball hacker.

INTRODUCTION

CODING AND COMPUTER SCIENCE

The title of this book is *Code This!*, but there are actually two things we're going to learn. One is the art of **figuring out** how to do things in general. That's called computer science. The other is the art of **explaining** how to do something in particular. That is called programming, or coding. We call them both "arts" because they require the same creativity you use when drawing, dancing, singing, or telling stories.

Why are they two different arts? Because in order to explain something clearly enough for a computer to understand, you first have to be able to think about it clearly to yourself. The computer is like a mirror for your mind: If your thoughts don't make sense, the reflection won't make sense either.

And like other kinds of art, computer science and computer programming use different tools. If you're in a painting class, you use brushes and easels. If you're in band or orchestra, you use a musical instrument. It's the same with different kinds of computer arts. In computer science puzzles, your tools include logic and math. In computer programming, you write specific directions called code.

Computer science and coding are like puzzle pieces—they're different from each other, but they fit together to solve a problem.

PRACTICAL APPLICATIONS

What can we do with computer science?

Almost anything! The world increasingly relies on computers—to send and receive information through the internet, to use mobile phones, to watch television, and to play games. Even this book you're holding right now was written on a computer.

The doctor is in ... the computer? Computer scientists write programs that help doctors learn about diseases and how to cure them. Special programs can even help doctors to do surgery.

Computer science keeps more than just computers running. Many cars have motors and other features that rely on computer programs.

Sometimes the best way to learn about Earth is to study space. Computer programmers write code that helps satellites look deep into space to grab photos. They also control the machines that scramble over faraway surfaces, like on Mars, or fly close to the atmosphere of other planets in our solar system.

Do you like to rock out, or are you more of the classical type? Hip-hop, salsa, or jazz—if you're hearing music, you're hearing it courtesy of a computer. It takes special code to make your favorite song sound perfectly in tune.

Computers are hard at work, even when we are relaxing. People called software engineers program computers to make your favorite movies and video games come to life.

THINKING LOGICALLY

WHAT IS LOGIC?

Good coders always consider logic when they tackle a problem. Logic is just thinking about something in a way that makes sense. When you're getting dressed in the morning, you wouldn't put your shoes on before your socks, would you? That wouldn't make sense. If the goal is to have your socks on under your shoes, it's more logical—that is, it makes more sense—to put your socks on first.

COMPUTER LOGIC

Since the idea behind programming a computer is to write directions in a way that gets the computer to do something, accomplish a goal, then it helps to think about how to write those directions in a way that makes sense. **Hey, that's logic!** So, doing logic problems is a big part of computer science.

Do computers use logic? In a way, they do. In fact, the tiny electronic parts that make up computers are put together in a way that uses a special kind of logic.

But computer logic is different from human logic. A human brain is creative. It's also great at sensing the world around us and taking all of what it senses into consideration as it tries to figure out what to do next. So, ultimately, it takes the human mind to dream up the best way to solve a problem, and to tell the computer how to do it.

My computer will need socks and shoes if it's going to "run" my program!

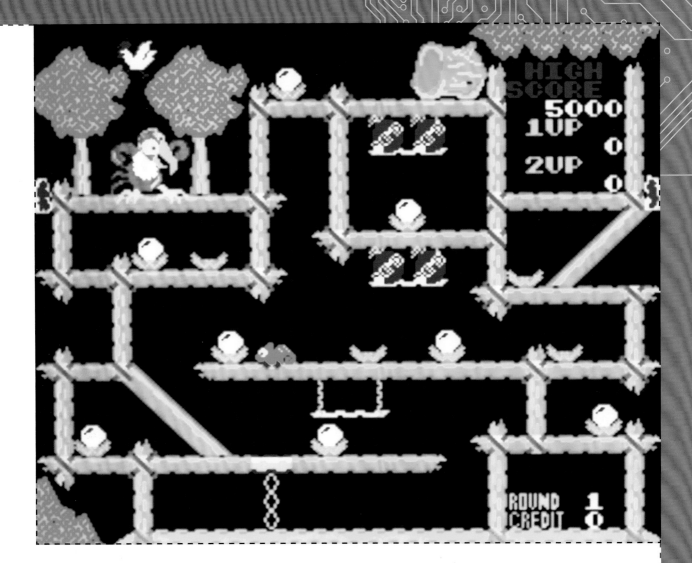

WHY DO COMPUTERS NEED CODE?

A computer is like any other kind of machine or tool. A screwdriver won't drive a screw into a board by itself. It takes a person to pick up the screwdriver, point the correct end of the screwdriver toward the screw, line up the tip of the screwdriver with the slot on the screw, put the end into the slot, push down, turn the screw in the right direction, and stop when the screw is all the way in.

Now, you'd probably do all of that without thinking about it too much. But if you didn't do all of those things, and all of those things in the right order, the screwdriver wouldn't be able to do its job correctly—or at all! It's the same with a computer. Computer scientists think about how to write the directions so the computer works to do a task completely and efficiently, and as quickly as possible. If they write them correctly, the right kind of computer will be able to do almost any kind of job!

TRY IT OUT

MEET THE FROGBOT

Meet the _Frontus jumpus_ robotic frog (not a real frog or a real robot). This robot is a very simple computer. It can only jump forward—and it can only jump one hop at a time. And, like all computers, it doesn't do anything it's not programmed to do!

Frogbot (_Frontus jumpus_)

Super springy legs and feet help frogbot leap long distances.

Frogbot can't turn unless it's instructed to.

Its eyes and antenna can sense obstacles.

Unlike a real frog, frogbot can only do what it's programmed to do.

Frogbot can only complete one command at a time: It can move forward or it can rotate, not both.

MEET THE BLOCK COMMANDS

Beginning computer coders learn to write code by using what we'll call block commands. A command is an instruction that a computer follows. In this book, a block command looks like this:

> ## JUMP FORWARD

To write code, you simply pile blocks together in a list. Frogbot will follow the commands beginning at the top, and ending at the bottom.

START
JUMP FORWARD
TURN LEFT
JUMP FORWARD
TURN RIGHT
JUMP FORWARD
JUMP FORWARD
TURN RIGHT
JUMP FORWARD
TURN LEFT
JUMP FORWARD
STOP

START

STOP

If frogbot needs to reach the flower, how would you use the command blocks?

STEP 2

If you wanted frogbot to jump one more space to the flower, you'd add a second command block.

JUMP FORWARD

So, the whole code would be:

START

JUMP FORWARD

JUMP FORWARD

STOP

STEP 1

If you use the command block:

JUMP FORWARD

Frogbot would move forward one space.

Jumping sounds like fun!

TRY IT OUT

CONTINUED

How can you use the command blocks to help frogbot cross the stream?

START

STOP

If you wrote:

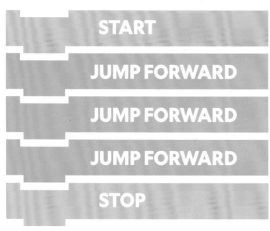

START

JUMP FORWARD

JUMP FORWARD

JUMP FORWARD

STOP

That's correct! To get the whole way across the stream, frogbot has to move three hops. So, you have to tell it to jump forward three times.

Let's add a new command block:

TURN LEFT

When frogbot reaches this command block, it will turn left, like this:

So this:

STOP

Looks like this:

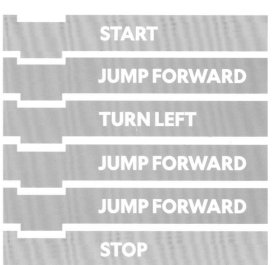

START

JUMP FORWARD

TURN LEFT

JUMP FORWARD

JUMP FORWARD

STOP

Try it again

Write the code to get frogbot across the stream and to the flower. Remember that frogbot can't do two commands at once. It can jump, or it can turn, but it can't do both at the same time.

START

Hint: There are 8 steps.

Jump to it.

CODE TOOLBOX

START

JUMP FORWARD

TURN LEFT

TURN RIGHT

STOP

HERE'S THE ANSWER:
START
JUMP FORWARD
JUMP FORWARD
TURN LEFT
JUMP FORWARD
TURN RIGHT
JUMP FORWARD
JUMP FORWARD
JUMP FORWARD
STOP

STOP

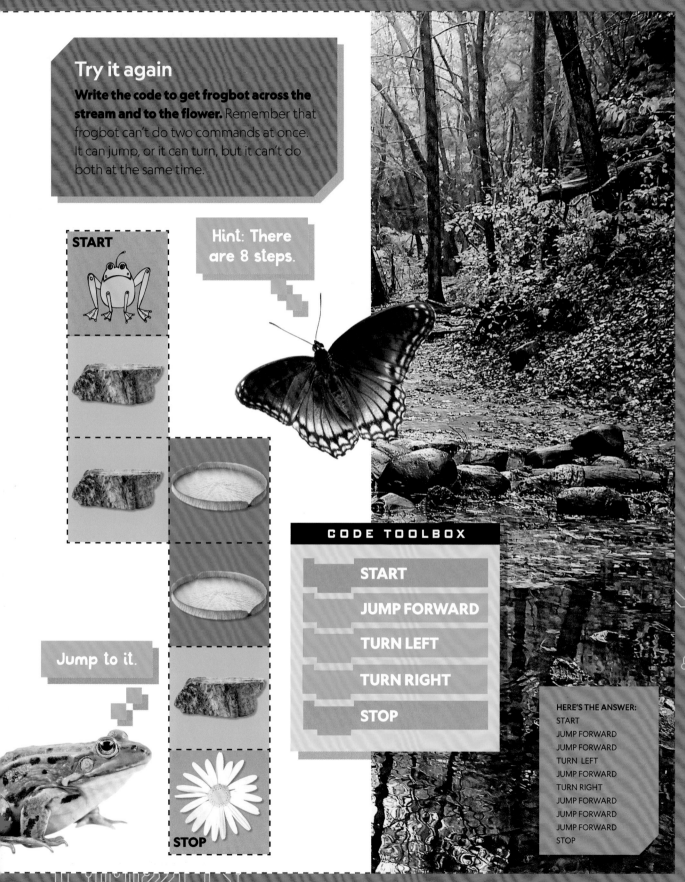

WELCOME TO THE
CODER CREW

>> **Ready for your mission?**

MEET CODY

Imagine that National Geographic's whiz engineers created Cody, an all-purpose robot that will help Explorers in the field with…well, just about anything. Cody is flexible, sturdy, and packed with gadgets. It can easily get to all the difficult and dangerous places where Explorers collect data.

I spotted you immediately!

I totally blend in.

No need to haul samples to a lab! Cody can process anything it needs to in its belly.

If you need it, Cody has it! Cody's arm gadgets include a flashlight, tools, and more.

Cody can go anywhere, thanks to its extendable all-terrain wheels. It can even be customized to take on water challenges!

Cody was built with many features that help it blend into its surroundings, including an extendable neck!

THE CATCH

Whenever an Explorer needs a hand, Cody's there to help. Unfortunately, it's very particular about the details. It can't simply collect a rare type of bacteria from a volcano. It needs step-by-step instructions on where to go, how to collect the bacteria, what bacteria to collect, and how to get back to the Explorers.

Even more unfortunately, Explorers are busy folks with a lot of cool stuff on their minds. They rarely give Cody the instructions it needs, which makes it want to totally short-circuit. That's where YOU come in. **Welcome to the Coder Crew.**

Does not compute.

➤➤ YOUR MISSION

THROUGHOUT THIS BOOK, YOUR JOB IS TO GIVE CODY THE INSTRUCTIONS IT NEEDS TO COMPLETE THE EXPLORERS' MISSIONS.

You'll need to break down each of the Nat Geo Explorers' big tasks into smaller ones that you can give Cody instructions for. Then you'll need to instruct Cody on what to do. Are you up for the challenge? The Nat Geo Explorers are relying on YOU for some of the toughest, trickiest, most awesome missions on Earth.

There are lots of different kinds of puzzles in this book—some will be easier, and some will be a little more challenging. Don't be afraid to try them all!

Real computer coders have something in common with kids—both learn by trying new things and making mistakes.

And here's a hint that might surprise you— if you're *really* stuck, **go find the answer in the back!** That's right. Look at the solution. But here's the catch: Don't just look at the answer, really *examine* it. Ask yourself: *Why* is this the right answer? *How* could you get that answer? Work backward! Sometimes that's the best way to learn.

Ready to take on the challenge? OK! Let's *Code This!* ➤➤

>> 1 >>

CHAPTER 1
THE MYSTERIOUS CAVE

CODING CONCEPTS IN THIS CHAPTER:

ALGORITHMS **OPTIMIZATION** **CRYPTOLOGY**

DIRECTIONS **LOOPS**

THE CHALLENGE

>> FIND THE ARTIFACTS

OBJECTIVE: PROGRAM CODY TO EXPLORE A CAVE AND LOOK FOR ANCIENT ARTIFACTS.

THE SITUATION

Exploring a route used by people to trade goods for **hundreds of years,** the Explorers come upon a cave. Could there be some **artifacts** left from these travelers in the cave? No one knows what conditions are like in the cave, so it's **not safe for humans** to go exploring. But Cody's up to the task! How can the Explorers program Cody to find artifacts in the dark cave?

THERE'S NO TELLING HOW DEEP THIS CAVE IS, AND BATTERIES DON'T LAST FOREVER! YOU'LL HAVE TO PROGRAM CODY TO BE EFFICIENT.

CODING CONCEPT: ALGORITHMS

Mmm ...
Bananas.
That algorithm
looks yummy.

DECODE THE CONCEPT

Computers use **algorithms** to accomplish tasks. An algorithm is just a fancy word for a list of directions. You use algorithms all the time, and probably didn't even know it!

THERE ARE TWO BIG RULES FOR WRITING A GOOD ALGORITHM FOR A COMPUTER:

1. Write down every single step that the computer needs to do.

2. Write down all the steps in the right order.

Following these steps is a little like following a path. You need to travel in the right order to accomplish your goal.

ADA LOVELACE

The world's first computer algorithm was written by Ada Lovelace. She wrote a list of directions to be completed by a computer that hadn't even been invented yet! She's considered to be the world's first computer programmer.

TRY IT OUT

If you've ever baked a cake or made cookies, you've used an algorithm. If you don't follow the steps of a recipe in the right order, you're likely to end up with a kitchen catastrophe ... or at least something that doesn't taste very good!

But how do you know if you're writing a good algorithm? Computer coders don't just write a list of directions and hope it works. After they write an algorithm, they make sure all of the steps are there. If there are any steps missing, they go back and add them.

How to Make a Smoothie (Sort of)

Here are some steps that can be used to make a yummy fruit smoothie.

- PUT BANANA PIECES INTO THE BLENDER.
- GET A CUP OF YOUR FAVORITE FROZEN FRUIT.
- MEASURE OUT ½ CUP OF MILK OR YOGURT.
- PUT THE MILK OR YOGURT IN THE BLENDER.
- TURN THE BLENDER ON TO ITS HIGHEST SETTING.
- WAIT 3 OR 4 MINUTES, OR UNTIL SMOOTH.
- TAKE THE LID OFF THE BLENDER.
- DRINK THE SMOOTHIE.

But are all the steps really there?

Here are a few other steps that can be added to the algorithm. **Can you figure out where they should go?**

- TURN OFF THE BLENDER.
- PEEL A BANANA AND BREAK IT INTO PIECES.
- PUT THE LID ON THE BLENDER.
- PUT THE FRUIT INTO THE BLENDER.
- POUR THE SMOOTHIE INTO A GLASS.

Write your smoothie algorithm on a piece of paper. Add any additional steps you need to finish your fruity masterpiece!

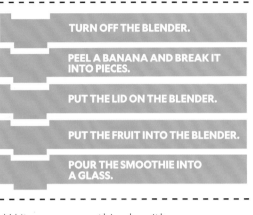

ALGORITHMS CONTINUES

CODING CONCEPT: ALGORITHMS

▶▶ TRY IT OUT

PROGRAM A FRIEND

Write an **algorithm** to help a friend drop a paper ball into a trash can.

CODE TOOLBOX

TAKE ONE STEP FORWARD

TURN TO THE LEFT

TURN TO THE RIGHT

OPEN YOUR HAND

RAISE YOUR ARM

WHAT YOU'LL NEED

- An empty trash can or bucket

- Tape

- A pillow or other soft object

- A piece of paper, wadded up into a ball

- Pencil and paper

- A friend

WHAT TO DO

1   STAND NEXT TO THE TRASH CAN.
Take five steps in one direction. Mark this spot on the floor with a piece of tape.

2   PLACE THE PILLOW about halfway between the tape and the trash can.

3   Using the commands in the toolbox, **WRITE AN ALGORITHM** (list of directions) that will cause your friend to walk from the tape, around the pillow, up to the trash can, and then drop the paper ball into the can.

4   GIVE YOUR FRIEND the ball of paper. Direct them to stand at the tape and close their eyes. Read your algorithm aloud one step at a time, with your friend performing each action. Your friend can **only** do what you say, and nothing else!

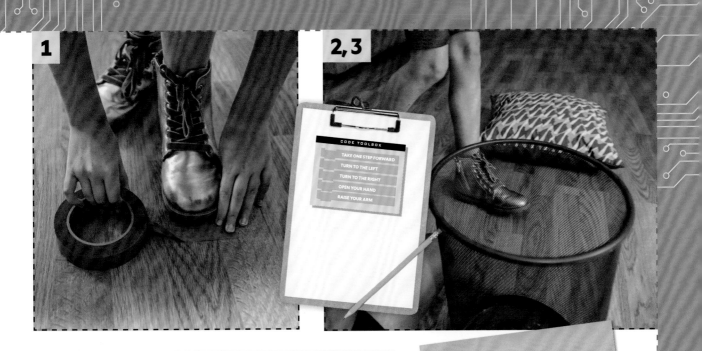

1

2,3

CODE TOOLBOX

TAKE ONE STEP FORWARD
TURN TO THE LEFT
TURN TO THE RIGHT
OPEN YOUR HAND
RAISE YOUR ARM

4

THINK ABOUT IT

Can you write an algorithm for ...
... getting ready for school?
... making yourself a sandwich?
What command blocks would
you use?

WHAT'S GOING ON?

We sometimes like to think that computers are
"smart"—and they are. But computers can't do
what the human brain does. If someone tells
you to throw a paper ball into a trash can, your
brain automatically figures out the steps you
need to do and makes you do them.
Computers can't do that.

PROBLEM SOLVE!

Did your algorithm work? Why or
why not? How would you change
it if there were two pillows in the
way instead of one?

CODING CONCEPT: OPTIMIZATION

DECODE THE CONCEPT

Computers can solve problems quickly. This is, in part, because of something called **optimization.** When coders write algorithms, they try to write them so that the computer can carry out the instructions in the best way possible.

Coders use a logic problem called the **Traveling Salesperson** to help them practice how to optimize the code they write.

This logic problem is way older than computers. The Traveling Salesperson problem asks the question, "How can I get to all of the stops I need to make in the most efficient way possible?"

It got its name from a time when there were traveling salespeople who would travel from town to town—and sometimes home to home—to try to sell their products. To do that, salespeople would want to visit all the possible customers using the shortest possible route. That way they could meet with more customers in the same amount of time. Sometimes the most efficient route is clear, but sometimes it's much harder to figure out.

CODING CONNECTION

One of the reasons that computer science can be tricky is that there's often more than one answer to a problem. What if the salesperson had to travel to 50 cities? 100? There might be a million possible answers, and it would take a long time to figure out the best one. So sometimes coders pick the answer that's not the best, but one that's good enough.

DID YOU KNOW?

This problem was first officially described in the 1800s by a mathematician named William Rowan Hamilton. A path that visits each of an area's points once is called a Hamiltonian path. (Unless it makes a loop, in which case it's called a Hamiltonian cycle.)

DON'T TRY THIS AT HOME!

Hamilton is also famous for carving mathematical equations into the Broome Bridge in Dublin, Ireland, on October 16, 1843. To honor the mathematician, people visit this graffiti every year on that date.

OPTIMIZATION CONTINUES ≫

CODING CONCEPT:
OPTIMIZATION

▶▶ TRY IT OUT

YOU BE THE TRAVELING EXPLORER

It's your turn to be the traveling explorer. You have some errands to do before dinner.

YOU HAVE TO:

1. drop off library books
2. go to the grocery store
3. mail a package at the post office

You need to visit each place once (and only once: You're in a hurry, remember), and you need to start from home and end up back there in time for dinner.

And let's say you have a little red wagon, so you don't need to worry about carrying anything.

Now, the places you need to be are scattered all over your neighborhood, like this. The numbers between each point show the time in minutes it takes to walk between each of them. What's the best route for you to take?

In which order will you go from place to place?

1. Leave home
2. STOP 1
(total time traveled so far = ?)
3. STOP 2
(total time traveled so far = ?)
4. STOP 3
(total time traveled so far = ?)
5. Return home
(total time for the whole trip = ?)

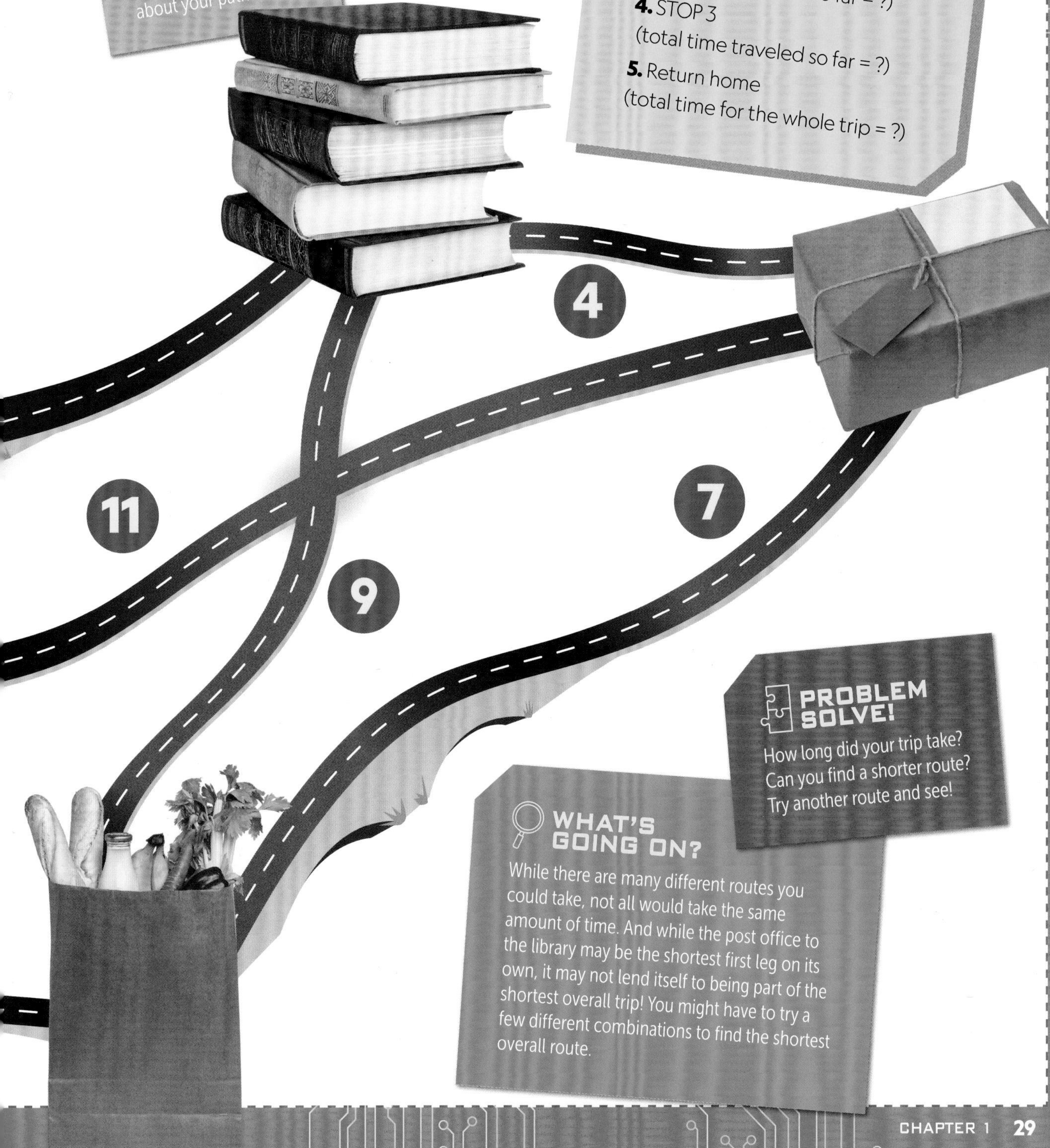

4

11

7

9

WHAT'S GOING ON?

While there are many different routes you could take, not all would take the same amount of time. And while the post office to the library may be the shortest first leg on its own, it may not lend itself to being part of the shortest overall trip! You might have to try a few different combinations to find the shortest overall route.

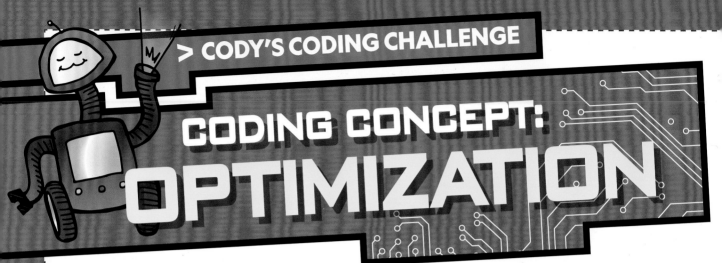

>> TRY IT OUT

CAVE EXPLORER CODY

OK, Coder Crew. Ready to help Cody tackle the cave?

The National Geographic Explorers have done their research. With the help of LIDAR, they have made a map of the rooms inside the first tunnel.

Each letter on the map represents a small room in the cave where there might be artifacts. The lines between the rooms represent paths that connect the rooms. The numbers represent the time in minutes it will take Cody to get from room to room. Cody has to get back to HQ before its batteries lose all their charge, so you want to program Cody to explore each room once (and only once), and then come back out of the tunnel in the shortest amount of time possible. **What would be the best path to program Cody to follow?**

WHAT TO DO

1 START at the room labeled A.

2 Decide **WHICH ROOM** Cody should go to next. Write down the number between these two rooms.

3 Decide which room Cody should go to next. Write down the number between these two rooms. **REPEAT** until Cody has been in all the rooms.

4 REMEMBER: Cody shouldn't go to any room more than once, and it has to finish at room A.

5 ADD ALL THE NUMBERS together. How long will your route take Cody to complete?

WHAT'S LIDAR?

LIDAR, or Light Detection and Ranging, is a remote-sensing method that uses laser lights to measure distances to Earth. The data from the light form an accurate 3D image of whatever you're scanning. That's handy when you're trying to map things you can't see easily from Earth's surface, like caves!

Hints: Cody is already facing room B.

Before you begin, think about different decisions you might make to pick a path.

Can there be more than one way to write the code?

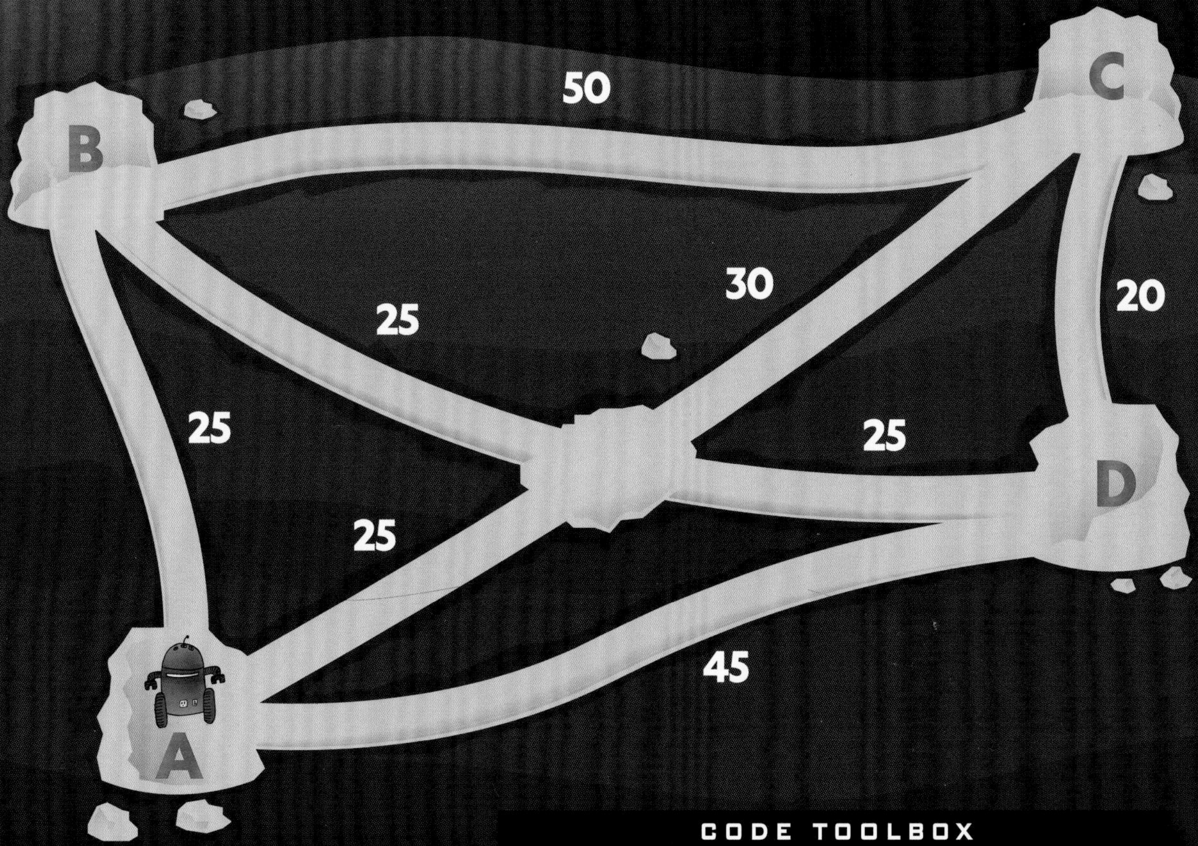

The diagram shows rooms connected by paths with the following distances:
B to C: 50
B (middle): 25
Middle to C area: 30
C to D: 20
A to B: 25
A (middle): 25
Middle to D: 25
A to D: 45

CODE TOOLBOX

MOVE FORWARD FOR 5 MINUTES

MOVE FORWARD FOR 10 MINUTES

TURN RIGHT

TURN LEFT

GO FURTHER!

After watching the footage from Cody's camera, the Explorers know that there's a cool artifact in each room. Now that Cody's back in room A, they want it to go and snap a picture of each artifact. Using the command blocks in the toolbox, plus the command block: Snap a Picture, can you write code for Cody to follow? Cody should move from room A to room B to room C.

CODING CONCEPT:
CRYPTOLOGY

DECODE THE CONCEPT

When computers send messages, such as emails, through the internet, they often need to be protected. After all, you wouldn't want everyone in the world knowing your business. But **cryptology**—the study of how to write and understand codes—is nothing new. People have been sending secret messages for as long as there have been people!

CODE BREAKERS

Code breakers—people who learn how to figure out ciphers—have changed the history of the world! Alan Turing and Gordon Welchman were able to break the Enigma code used by Germany in World War II, and members of the Native American Navajo tribe developed a code to use during the same war that proved to be nearly unbreakable.

Agent 001 reporting for duty.

SECRET CIPHERS

An important part of breaking ciphers is knowing the key. The key to this code is below.

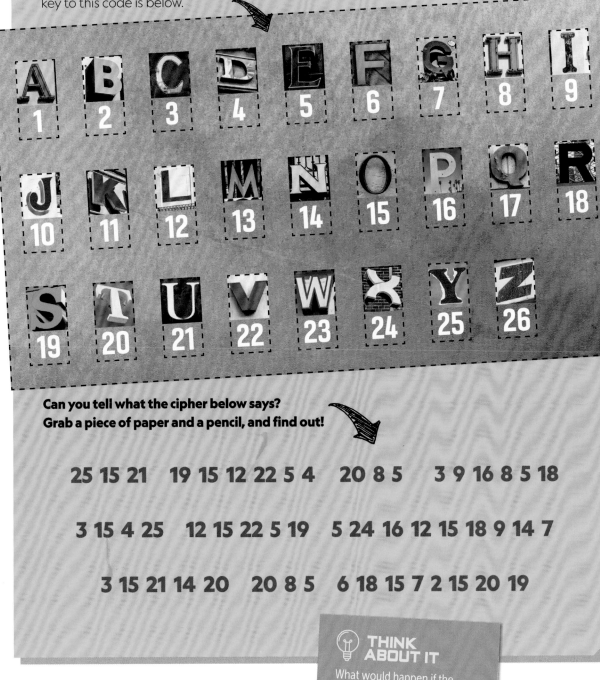

Can you tell what the cipher below says?
Grab a piece of paper and a pencil, and find out!

25 15 21   19 15 12 22 5 4   20 8 5   3 9 16 8 5 18

3 15 4 25   12 15 22 5 19   5 24 16 12 15 18 9 14 7

3 15 21 14 20   20 8 5   6 18 15 7 2 15 20 19

💡 **THINK ABOUT IT**

What would happen if the person who gets your message doesn't know the key?

CIPHERS CONTINUES >>

H'L OHMJ ADBZTRD H DZS RGQHLO.

CODING CONCEPT:
CRYPTOLOGY

▷▷ TRY IT OUT

SUBSTITUTION CIPHERS

One of the more difficult ciphers is called a **substitution cipher.** In this kind of cipher, one letter is changed with another. Both the person who sends the message and the person who receives the message need to have the key to discover the message .

IN THIS KEY, THE ALPHABET USED TO WRITE THE CIPHER IS MOVED ONE LETTER.

Normal:

A B C D E F G H I J K L M N O P Q R S T U V W X Y Z

Cipher:

Z A B C D E F G H I J K L M N O P Q R S T U V W X Y

Grab a piece of paper. **Can you write these messages below using the cipher alphabet in the second row?**

A GIRAFFE'S TONGUE IS BLACK!

BATS HAVE THUMBS!

Now can you decrypt these fun animal facts?

ZM NBSNOTR GZR SGQDD GDZQSR.

FNKCEHRG BZM KDZQM SN CN SQHBJR.

LZKD ODMFTHMR JDDO DFFR VZQL.

MN SVN SHFDQR' RSQHODR ZQD ZKHJD.

AQHFGS BNKNQR VZQM ZVZX OQDCZSNQR.

CODING CONCEPT: CRYPTOLOGY

>> TRY IT OUT

MAKE A CIPHER WHEEL

It can be hard to come up with a supersecret cipher. After all, just about anyone could guess a key that just shifted the letters of the alphabet by one letter. Use this cipher wheel to help generate hard-to-crack ciphers.

WHAT YOU'LL NEED

- Two paper plates
- Scissors
- Pencil or pen
- Single-hole punch or scissors
- Paper fastener

CODING CONNECTION

Lots of important information is sent to and from and stored on computers. Computer scientists study cryptology to learn how to protect this information. Learning about ciphers also helps coders write programs that read passwords.

THINK ABOUT IT

How many wheels would you need if you wrote a message in code, and then translated it into a second code?

WHAT TO DO

1 CUT ONE PAPER PLATE so that it's a smaller circle than the other.

2 FOLD EACH PAPER PLATE IN QUARTERS, so that it looks like a piece of pie.

MAKE A CIPHER WHEEL CONTINUES ≫

MAKE A CIPHER WHEEL

3

3 Use the hole punch or scissors to **PUNCH OR CUT A SMALL HOLE AT THE VERY END OF THE FOLDED PLATE.** Be careful not to make the hole too big. Unfold the plates.

4 USING THE IMAGE SHOWN ON PAGE 39 AS A GUIDE, place the small circle on top of the large circle. Write the alphabet on each wheel, evenly spaced around each wheel. You may wish to draw 26 dots evenly spaced around each circle so that they line up together across the small and large circle, then write in each letter.

5 Put the smaller wheel on top of the larger wheel. **FASTEN THE WHEELS TOGETHER** with the paper fastener.

4

12

BACK SIDE OF FASTENER

9

3

6

HOW TO USE YOUR CIPHER WHEEL

CHOOSE TWO LETTERS TO BE YOUR KEY. Remember, only you and the person you're sending the cipher to should know these letters! For example, you might choose the letters E and A.

FIND THE FIRST KEY LETTER (E) on the large wheel. Turn the inside wheel until the second key letter (A) is right below the first.

USE THE LETTERS ON THE INSIDE WHEEL TO WRITE YOUR CIPHER. For example, if the key letters are E and A, Cody's name (CODY) would be: YKZU.

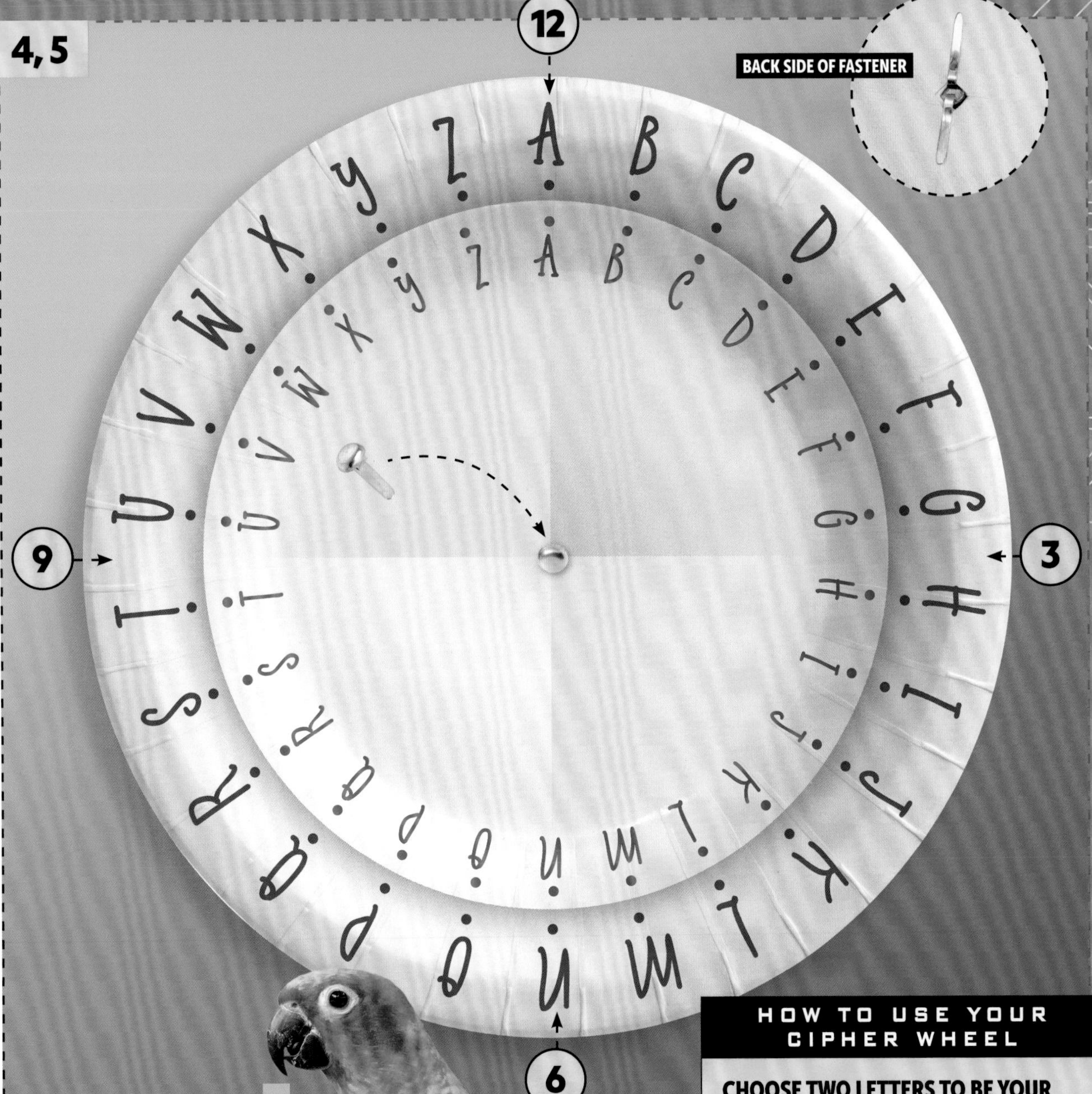

Tip: Put the letter A at 12 o'clock, and N at 6 o'clock. 3 o'clock should be between G and H, and 9 o'clock should be between T and U.

CODING CONCEPT: CRYPTOLOGY

>> TRY IT OUT

CAVE CODES

As Cody makes its way into the room labeled C, it comes upon some strange writing on the wall. It looks like a cipher. Can you figure out what it says?

E=A

PDA OPQZU
KB YWRAO
EO YWHHAZ
OLAHAKHKCU

Hints: To decode this kind of cipher, you need a pair of key letters.

You can use a cipher wheel or a pencil and paper to help you crack this code.

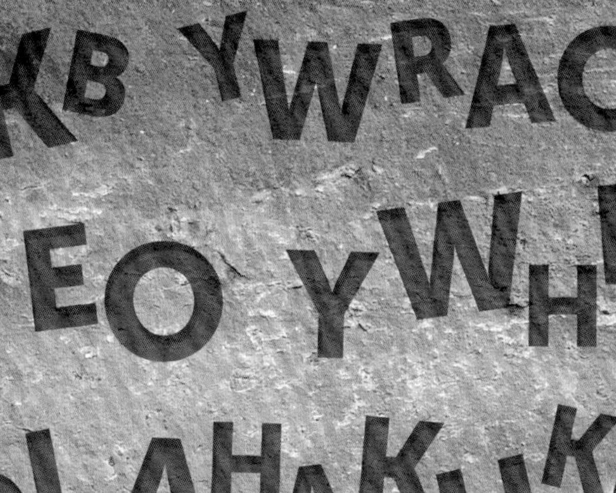

CODING CONCEPT:
DIRECTIONS

DECODE THE CONCEPT

You've probably worked your way through a maze, but have you ever really thought about all the different parts of a maze? **You can use the parts of a maze to understand how to write a maze-solving code!**

Who knew that mazes had parts? Me, that's who!

ENTRANCE

The starting point, or where you enter the maze from the outside

WALL

The barriers that you cannot pass through within the maze. The spaces between the walls form the paths.

PATH

A route you travel through a maze

DEAD END

A spot in the maze where a path comes to an end—you have no choice but to turn around and choose a different direction.

BACKTRACK

Turning around to try a new path

EXIT

The end point of the maze

JUNCTION

A point in the maze where paths branch off from each other or meet up with each other

SOLUTION

A successful path from the entrance to the exit

CODING CONCEPT:
DIRECTIONS

>>> TRY IT OUT

WHAT YOU'LL NEED

- Chalk, tape, or other materials for marking
- A big open area
- A friend to be the mousebot

MOUSEBOT ON THE MOVE!

Meet the *Mousus movus* robotic mouse (not a real mouse or a real robot). This robot is a very simple computer. It can do two things: It can move and it can rotate. But it can't do them at the same time. To get mousebot to turn in a new direction, you first need to program it to turn, then you need to program it to move forward in the new direction it is facing.

∧ = Go forward one space.
> = Turn right
< = Turn left

WHAT TO DO

1 COPY THE MAZE on the next page onto the big open area using tape or chalk.

2 Using only the blocks in the toolbox, **WRITE AN ALGORITHM** to get your mousebot through the maze.

3 Have your **MOUSEBOT STAND IN THE MAZE** at the area marked "Start."

4 FOLLOW YOUR ALGORITHM ONE STEP AT A TIME. Remember: You can't go through the maze walls! And you can't do more than one command at the same time.

FOLLOW THAT WALL!

People have always enjoyed solving mazes, including labyrinths, which are large mazes. Some labyrinths have hedges for walls. One plan for getting out of a labyrinth is called wall-following. There are two rules to follow:
1. Keep your right hand on the right wall at all times.
2. Make a right at every junction.

This strategy might take a long time, but it will work!

∧

>

<

Some programs have millions of lines of code. Why might coders prefer to use symbols like ∧ rather than writing out "Go forward one step"?

THINK ABOUT IT

Did you get your turns mixed up? Remember that when you're writing directions, you have to pretend that you are looking through the eyes of the robot. Otherwise, it's easy to make a left when you should make a right!

Stop

Right, now take a left.

Start

CODING CONCEPT:
LOOPS

I bet I can run loops around that mousebot!

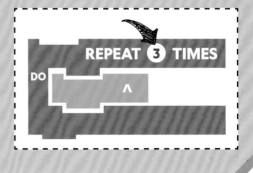

DECODE THE CONCEPT

Computers don't get bored doing the same thing over and over again, but people do! One of the shortcuts that coders take when writing directions is called a **loop.** A loop is any action that's done more than one time in a row. Clap your hands three times. You just did a loop!

THE COMMAND BLOCK FOR A LOOP LOOKS LIKE THIS:

REPEAT ● TIMES

DO

It's easy to use!

Just fit the command you want to do into the slot.

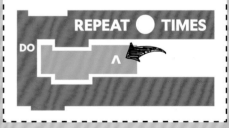

REPEAT ● TIMES

DO

^

Then write the number of times you want it done in the circle.

REPEAT ③ TIMES

DO

^

CODING CONNECTION

Sometimes coders will write loops into a program to save time and space. There's at least one loop inside almost every computer program. Sometimes there are loops in loops—these are called nested loops. Loops save coders lots of time, but they can sometimes make programs run more slowly.

≫ TRY IT OUT

Help mousebot reach the toadstool.

On a piece of paper, write an algorithm using the directional command blocks in the toolbox for mousebot to reach the toadstool.

Now write the algorithm again. This time you can use the loop block.

Use a coin or other object to try both of your algorithms on the board below.

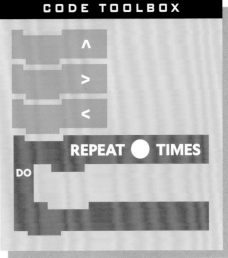

CODE TOOLBOX

∧

>

<

REPEAT ● TIMES

DO

🧩 PROBLEM SOLVE!

How many steps are in each algorithm? Which algorithm was shorter to write?

🔍 WHAT'S GOING ON?

When the mousebot encountered the algorithm with the loop, it knew to repeat the command within the loop, and it knew how many times to repeat it. Every time mousebot finished a loop, it moved on to the next command in the algorithm.

▤ CODING CONNECTION

Computer programs use lots of code. Smartphone and tablet apps might run on a hundred thousand lines, but some of the software that makes a computer work can have more than 50 million lines! It takes large teams of people working together to write that much code.

Start

Stop

CODING CONCEPT: LOOPS

>> TRY IT OUT

CODY AND THE LABYRINTH

After exploring the first tunnel, Cody returned with a cool cipher. After studying the map some more, the Explorers think there might be some interesting crystals in the second tunnel. Take a look at the cave map. Can you **write an algorithm using the command blocks** in the toolbox to get Cody to the room deep inside the cave? Write your code, then use a coin or other object to try it out on page 49. Did it work?

You don't want to disturb the spiders. Cody should avoid them!

Remember: Λ means move forward 1 space.

The loop command block looks like it might come in handy!

Start

CODE TOOLBOX

∧

>

<

REPEAT ● TIMES

DO

Stop

THE MYSTERIOUS CAVE

OBJECTIVE: FIND AND PHOTOGRAPH ALL 10 ARTIFACTS AND RETURN TO THE CAVE ENTRANCE USING THE SHORTEST ALGORITHM POSSIBLE.

OK, Coder Crew. You've learned a lot in this chapter about algorithms, efficiency, and loops. It's time to put it all together and send Cody into the cave to see what artifacts it can find and photograph. Grab a piece of paper and a pencil to **write out your algorithm** using the **commands in the toolbox.** Then grab a coin or other small object to represent Cody and try out your algorithm on the map!

CODE TOOLBOX

- ∧
- >
- <
- ∨
- REPEAT ● TIMES
- DO
- TAKE PHOTO

Don't forget: Cody needs to return to the cave entrance once it's done photographing the 10 artifacts in the cave, and it can't go through the gray blocks.

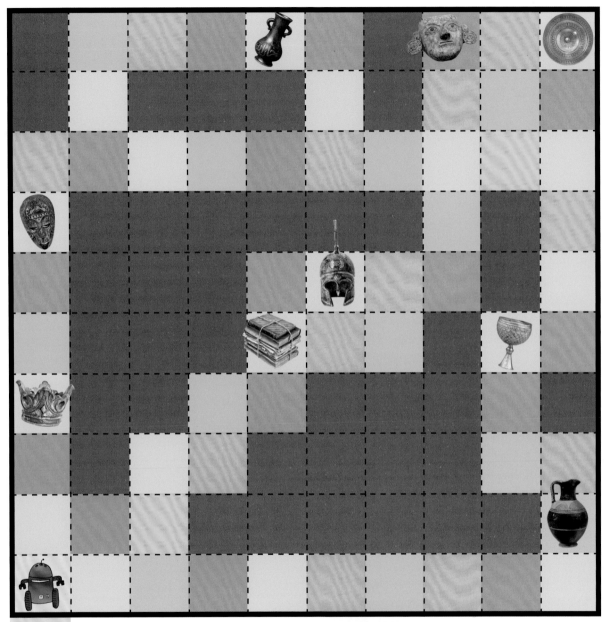

Entrance

Hint: Remember Cody can only do one action at a time: It can move, it can turn, or it can take a photo.

CHAPTER 2

DEEP-SEA SURPRISES

CODING CONCEPTS IN THIS CHAPTER:

CONSTRAINTS   DEBUGGING   BINARY CODE   BINARY SEARCH

THE CHALLENGE

OBJECTIVE: PROGRAM CODY TO HELP THE EXPLORERS DO SOME DEEP-SEA EXPLORATION.

THE SITUATION

The ocean floor can be a **dark and dangerous** place. Scientists often use robotically controlled vehicles to explore the deepest part of the ocean and to see what kinds of interesting animals live there. The National Geographic Explorers want to take a look down into the ocean depths. How can you program Cody to help the Explorers on their deep-sea expedition?

CODING CONCEPT:
CONSTRAINTS

DECODE THE CONCEPT

One of the things that coders must consider when they write computer programs are **constraints.** A constraint is anything that might keep a solution from working, or might keep it from working well. Try to tie your shoe. How long does it take? Add the constraint of not being able to use your thumbs, and then try to tie your shoe again. How does this change the solution?

You can practice working with constraints by solving this logic problem:

Three frogs and three toads sit on seven stones in a pond. The frogs on the left three stones would like to sit on the three stones on the right. The toads on the right would like to sit on the three stones on the left. Each animal can only hop one hop at a time, they can only hop forward, and they can't share a stone with another toad or frog. Each stone can only hold one animal at a time. **Can you figure out how to move the frogs and toads so that they switch sides?**

CONSTRAINTS CONTINUES

CODING CONCEPT:
CONSTRAINTS

>> TRY IT OUT

WHAT YOU'LL NEED

- A piece of paper and a pencil or pen

- Six small objects, like coins or blocks—with three of one kind and three of another to symbolize the frogs and toads

HOP TO IT!

Instead of frogs and toads, you can use objects to work out a solution to the problem on the previous page. Can you use logic to help two groups of objects switch sides?

I'm more of a howler than a hopper.

CODING CONNECTION

Most coding problems have at least one constraint—and constraints can make it a little trickier to find solutions. Thinking about constraints before trying to solve a problem can save a lot of time later, though!

MORE THAN A MATHEMATICIAN

Richard Guy, one of the people who helped to create this problem, turned 100 years old in 2016. Even after turning 100, he still goes to work every day, and he enjoys hiking and mountain climbing.

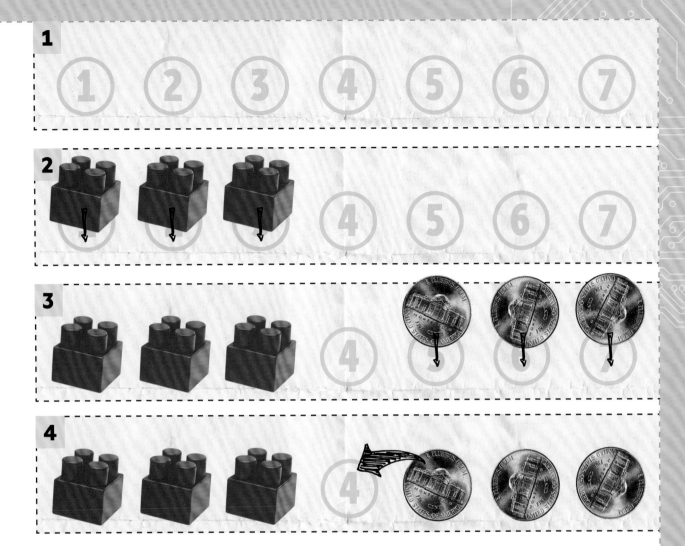

WHAT TO DO

1 DRAW SEVEN CIRCLES on the paper in a row like this. Number the circles 1 through 7. These seven circles will be the stones in the pond.

2 PUT THREE OF THE SAME OBJECT ON CIRCLES 1, 2, AND 3. These will represent the frogs in the pond.

3 PUT THE OTHER THREE OBJECTS ON CIRCLES 5, 6, AND 7. These represent the toads.

4 JUMP! Use the circles and objects to figure out how the frogs and toads can jump from rock to rock until the frogs are on circles 5, 6, and 7, and the toads are on circles 1, 2, and 3.

5 IF YOUR SOLUTION DOESN'T WORK, THAT'S OK! Just try again!

WHAT'S GOING ON?

Sometimes thinking about solving a problem means figuring out what not to do. Did you try a solution that didn't work? Did it include a move that ended with two frogs or two toads on rocks right next to each other? Once you identify what parts of solutions don't work, it's often easier to come up with one that does work!

THINK ABOUT IT

What constraints are there in this problem? How would the solution be different if there were no constraints? What if there were more constraints?

CODING CONCEPT:
CONSTRAINTS

>> TRY IT OUT

SPECIAL DELIVERY

Every journey begins with a single step.
And in this case, it begins with a problem! The Explorers have to get all of their supplies from shore out to their home base—a boat anchored out in the ocean. To do this, they plan on taking a smaller boat in multiple trips. Finally, they have just three things left to take:

The Explorers' picnic basket

The Expedition's official mascots: a cat and a dog

Hints: What are the constraints in this problem? What are some of the pairings that won't work on the boat? What are some that will work on the boat?

The Explorers are anxious to get started on their expedition. How can they program Cody to get all three things out to the home-base boat?

Write an algorithm that will get everything to the boat.

THERE ARE A FEW THINGS YOU NEED TO KNOW ABOUT THE SUPPLY TRIPS, THOUGH:

1. There is room for only three things in the boat—and one of those things has to be Cody, because the Explorers can remotely use it to steer the boat.

2. If the dog is left with the picnic basket, he will nab a few sandwiches.

3. The cat's super picky, and won't eat the food, but she and the dog can't be left alone together because they don't get along very well (at all!).

CODING CONCEPT: DEBUGGING

DECODE THE CONCEPT

Sometimes coders write code that, well, doesn't work. And that's okay! It happens all the time—a piece of code just doesn't work the way it's supposed to. A **bug** is a mistake in code. **Debugging** is finding mistakes in code ... and then fixing those mistakes.

Coders don't just guess when they're debugging—they have a plan, or **strategy.** One easy strategy to use when debugging is to ask yourself these three questions:

1. What happens when you run the code?

2. What *should* happen? (Instead of what *did* happen.)

3. What does this mean?

This will tell you what kind of mistake you're looking for.

Get a pencil, a piece of paper, and a ruler and try it!

There might be a bug in my travel plans.

TRY IT OUT

WHAT YOU'LL NEED

- A piece of paper
- A pencil
- A ruler

Let's go back to frogbot. It's been improved! Frogbot has been changed a little bit so that it can hold a pencil.

Did you catch it? Here's a hint: Put yourself in frogbot's shoes, and see things from its perspective.

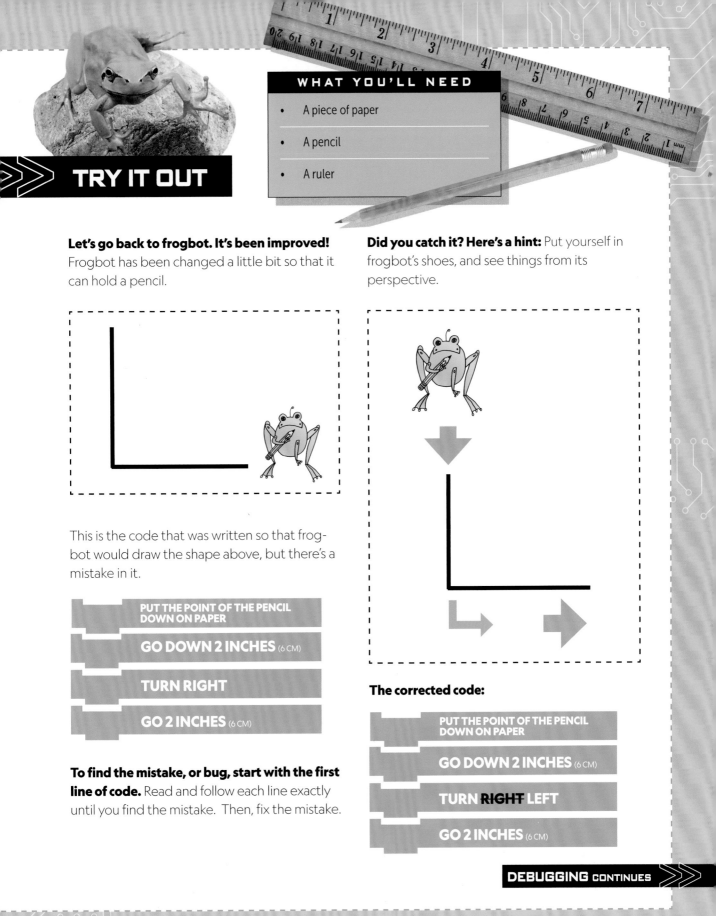

This is the code that was written so that frogbot would draw the shape above, but there's a mistake in it.

PUT THE POINT OF THE PENCIL DOWN ON PAPER

GO DOWN 2 INCHES (6 CM)

TURN RIGHT

GO 2 INCHES (6 CM)

To find the mistake, or bug, start with the first line of code. Read and follow each line exactly until you find the mistake. Then, fix the mistake.

The corrected code:

PUT THE POINT OF THE PENCIL DOWN ON PAPER

GO DOWN 2 INCHES (6 CM)

TURN **RIGHT** LEFT

GO 2 INCHES (6 CM)

DEBUGGING CONTINUES

> YOUR TURN

CODING CONCEPT:
DEBUGGING

>> TRY IT OUT

CUP-STACKING CODE DEBUGGING

Have you ever gotten a homework answer incorrect, and then gone back to figure out where you went wrong? Then you've already practiced debugging! Keep going by finding out what's wrong with the code in this game.

WHAT YOU'LL NEED

- 8 plastic drink cups

- A large piece of paper

- A pen

THOMAS EDISON

No one is quite sure why errors in computer programs are called "bugs," but the term has been around since long before there were computers. Even Thomas Edison—who worked in the late 1800s and early 1900s—called the problems he found in his inventions bugs.

In the early days of computers, parts were big enough to actually trap insects. There's been at least one record of a moth getting caught in a computer and causing the computer to not work correctly!

WHAT TO DO

1 TURN ONE OF THE CUPS UPSIDE DOWN AND TRACE ITS MOUTH on one edge of the paper. This will make a circle.

2 MOVE THE CUP OVER so that when you trace it the next time, the edge of the next circle will just touch the first.

3 REPEAT UNTIL THERE ARE FIVE CIRCLES in a single row across the paper. Number them 1, 2, 3, 4, and 5.

4 PLACE THE STACK OF 6 CUPS UPSIDE DOWN to the left of circle one.

5 ON THE NEXT PAGE, READ THE CODE IN EACH LINE OF THE TABLE. The picture in the second column shows what the cups should look like after you follow all the code. Follow the code exactly to see if the code works.

5

Here's an example: the code for a row of cups that looks like this ...

... would look like this:

∧ > > > > ∨ < < < < <

∧ > > > ∨ < < <

∧ > ∨ <

CODE TOOLBOX

∧	Pick up a cup
>	Move right one circle
<	Move left one circle
∨	Put the cup down
T	Flip the cup over

DEBUGGING CONTINUES

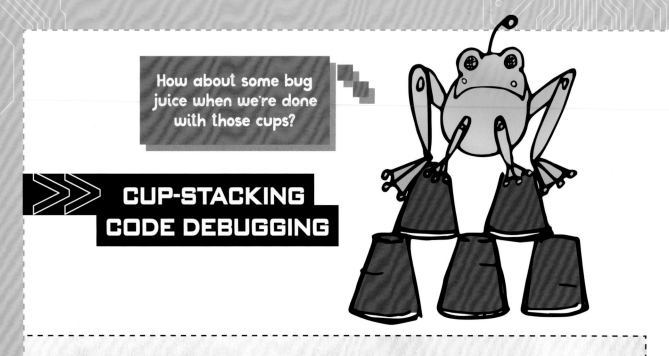

How about some bug juice when we're done with those cups?

» CUP-STACKING CODE DEBUGGING

Is the code for this stack correct? Try it and see! Start with the cups right-side up.

CODE

Λ > > > > > V < < < < <

Λ > > > > V < < < <

Λ > > > V < < <

Λ > V <

CORRECT EXECUTION

When you followed this code, did your stack look like this? If not, can you spot the bug in the code?

CODE TOOLBOX

Λ   Pick up a cup

\>   Move right one circle

<   Move left one circle

V   Put the cup down

T   Flip the cup over

WHAT'S GOING ON?

Computers don't make mistakes—coders do! But coders have something that computers don't—a brain. It takes a human brain to go through code to find and fix mistakes. That's why debugging is so important.

CODE

∧ > > > > ∨ < < < <
∧ > > > > ∨ < < < <
∧ > > > ∨ < < <
∧ > > ∨ < <
∧ > ∨ <
∧ > > > > T ∨ < < < <
∧ > > > T ∨ < < <
∧ > T ∨ <

CORRECT EXECUTION

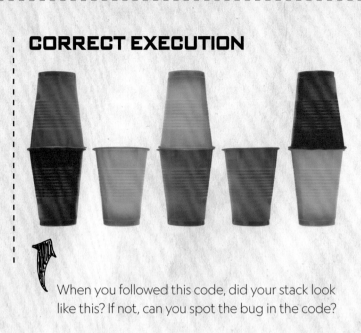

When you followed this code, did your stack look like this? If not, can you spot the bug in the code?

CODE

∧ > > > > > ∨ < < < < <
∧ > > > > ∨ < < < <
∧ > > > T ∨ < < <
∧ > > T ∨ < <
∧ > ∨ <
∧ > > > > ∨ < < < <
∧ > > T ∨ < <

CORRECT EXECUTION

When you followed this code, did your stack look like this? If not, can you spot the bug in the code?

THINK ABOUT IT

This is a short code, but what if you had a very long one? What if it were 100 lines? More? How would you go about finding a bug?

⊙ GO FURTHER!

What would the code look like for ...
... a tower that's four cups tall?
... a pyramid that has five cups in its bottom row?
... a cup creation that's all your own?

Try it and see!

CODING CONCEPT:
DEBUGGING

>> TRY IT OUT

CODY MISSES THE MARK

The National Geographic Explorers have used sonar to visualize the cold, dark seafloor. They programmed Cody to dive deep into the ocean's depths to photograph the ocean's floor. But it appears that Cody missed the mark! Knowing that Cody started the first two steps correctly (you could see it from the boat), can you debug this code so that it goes to the correct spot?

MOVE FORWARD

TURN LEFT

MOVE FORWARD

TURN RIGHT

MOVE FORWARD

TURN LEFT

MOVE FORWARD

TURN RIGHT

MOVE FORWARD

MOVE FORWARD

WHAT'S SONAR?

People use sonar (SOund Navigation and Ranging) to help them find their way around underwater or to identify objects that are deep under the surface. Sonar sensors send sound waves into the water, and they time how long it takes the waves to return after they've bounced off an object. People aren't the only creatures to use sound waves to find things—animals such as bats and whales have their own echolocation abilities.

Hint: What questions can you ask yourself to help you debug code that's not working right?

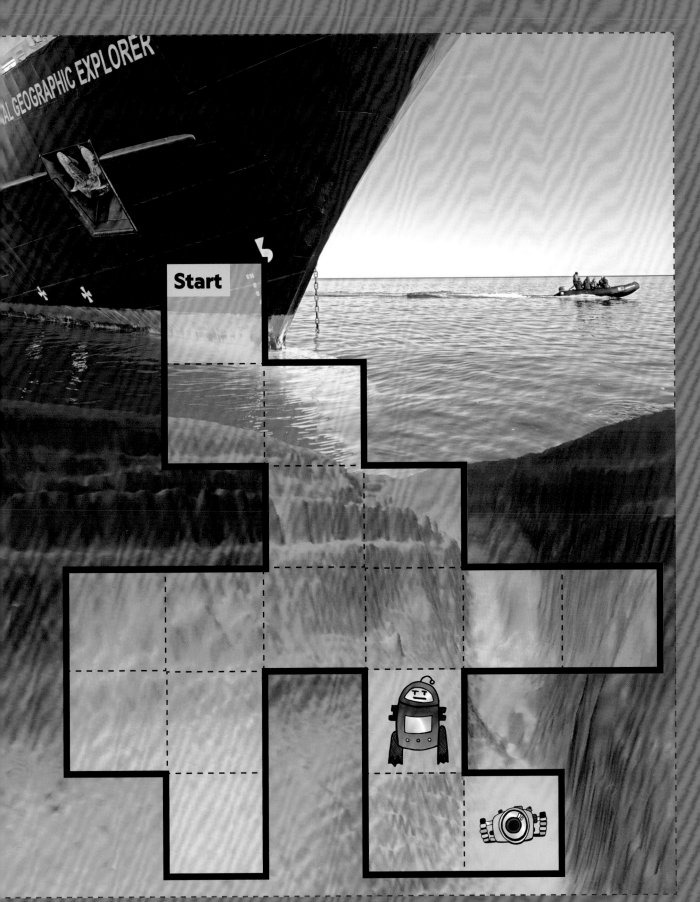

Start

CODING CONCEPT: BINARY CODE

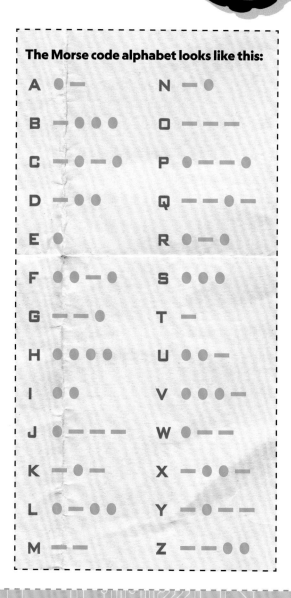

DECODE THE CONCEPT

Computers take the instructions written in words by coders and change them into what's called **binary code.** There are lots of different kinds of binary codes, but they all have one thing in common—they have just two parts.

THE "BI" IN BINARY MEANS TWO— JUST LIKE THERE ARE TWO WHEELS ON A BICYCLE.

Morse code is a kind of binary code. All the letters in the Morse code alphabet are made up of only two things: dots and dashes.

One of the coolest things about Morse code is that you can make the short and long parts using light! **Try it for yourself!**

The Morse code alphabet looks like this:

A	● —	N	— ●
B	— ● ● ●	O	— — —
C	— ● — ●	P	● — — ●
D	— ● ●	Q	— — ● —
E	●	R	● — ●
F	● ● — ●	S	● ● ●
G	— — ●	T	—
H	● ● ● ●	U	● ● —
I	● ●	V	● ● ● —
J	● — — —	W	● — —
K	— ● —	X	— ● ● —
L	● — ● ●	Y	— ● — —
M	— —	Z	— — ● ●

WHAT YOU'LL NEED

- Pencil and paper
- Two copies of the Morse code alphabet
- A flashlight
- A friend

WHAT TO DO

1 WRITE A TWO- OR THREE-WORD MESSAGE on the paper.

2 CHANGE EACH LETTER OF THE MESSAGE INTO MORSE CODE using the alphabet on the facing page.

3 USE A FLASHLIGHT in a dim room to send your code to someone else!

1 Write your secret message.

2
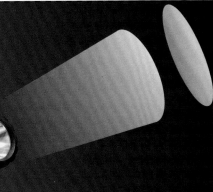

3
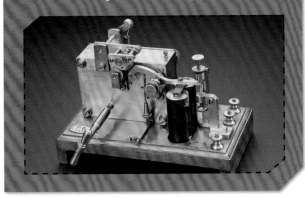

A DOT IS ONE QUICK FLASH OF THE LIGHT OR ONE QUICK TAP SOUND.

A DASH IS A FLASH OF THE LIGHT OR A TAP SOUND THAT IS THREE TIMES AS LONG AS A DOT.

MORSE CODE

Before telephones, people sent telegrams using Morse code. A person would take a message into a telegram office and give it to the operator. The operator would change the message into Morse code and tap it into a machine. The signal would travel through long wires to an operator on the other end, who would change the Morse code into a message that used the regular alphabet.

WHAT'S GOING ON?

If you've ever sent a text or email using a computer or smartphone, then you know that sending messages can be pretty easy—just type and press Send! But what's going on inside the computer is a lot like what used to happen in telegrams sent by Morse code. The code inside a computer or smartphone takes the message you type and changes it into a message that another computer can understand. It then sends your message to another computer that changes it back into a form another person can read!

THINK ABOUT IT

Can you think of another way besides light or sound to use Morse code to send messages?

BINARY CODE CONTINUES >>

CODING CONCEPT: BINARY CODE

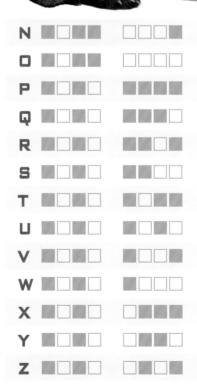

Hey, I'm two colors, too!

DECODE THE CONCEPT

Some computers use a code that is a bit like Morse code. Its official name is American Standard Code for Information Interchange, but you can just call it by its nickname, **ASCII** (pronounced AS-key).

ASCII letters are made of eight boxes. Some are colored in, and some are open. The ASCII alphabet looks like this:

A ■□□■ ■■■□
B ■□□■ ■■□□
C ■□□□ ■■□□
D ■□□■ □□□□
E ■□□■ □□□□
F ■□□□ ■□□□
G ■□□■ □□□□
H ■□□■ □■■■
I ■□□■ □□□■
J ■□□■ □□■□
K ■□□■ □□■■
L ■□□■ □□□□
M ■□□■ □□□■

N ■□□■ □□□■
O ■□□■ □□□□
P ■□□□ ■■■■
Q ■□□□ ■■■□
R ■□□■ ■□□□
S ■□□■ ■□□□
T ■□□■ ■□□■
U ■□□■ ■□□■
V ■□□■ ■□□■
W ■□□■ ■□□□
X ■□□■ □■□□
Y ■□□■ □□□■
Z ■□□■ □■□□

TRY IT OUT

WHAT YOU'LL NEED

- Pencil

- Paper

CODE TOOLBOX

- Open
- Closed

Can you write your name in ASCII? Grab a piece of paper and write your name in a line going from top to bottom. That's how a computer would read the code. Then, use the ASCII chart to draw the correct boxes for each letter.

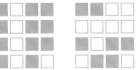

Here's how Cody would spell its name:

What is being spelled with these ASCII letters?

CODING CONCEPT: BINARY SEARCH

DECODE THE CONCEPT

We use computers to help us find the answers to problems all the time. Did you ever wonder how computers can find the answers so quickly? One type of algorithm that computers use to find information is called a **binary search.** Binary searches, like binary code, rely on the power of two. Let's see how!

DID YOU EVER PLAY "GUESS MY NUMBER"? In this game, one person thinks of a number, and the other tries to guess it.

For example, two friends decide to play this game. They decide that the rules of the game are:

1. The number has to be between 1 and 10.

2. After every incorrect guess, the person thinking of the number has to say whether their number is higher or lower.

If the correct number is 7, it might go something like this:

At the beginning of the game, any number between 1 and 10 could be the right answer.

After the first guess, only numbers higher than 3 can be correct: 4, 5, 6, 7, 8, 9, or 10.

After the next guess of 9, only 4, 5, 6, 7, or 8 could be right. Each time the number of right answers is cut into two parts until only the right answer (7) is left!

CODING CONNECTION

Some kinds of binary search code are used to quickly sort through a database. Databases are large pools of information. Some of the world's largest databases help us to shop on the internet, to watch videos online, and even to contact each other through email or phone.

CODING CONCEPT: BINARY SEARCH

>> TRY IT OUT

CODY COMMUNICATION

To figure out the meaning of Cody's flag, read each statement in the binary search tree. If the statement is true, follow the YES line. If the statement is false, follow the NO line. Keep going until the path ends!

FLAG HAS MORE THAN ONE COLOR
- Yes
- No

FLAG HAS HORIZONTAL (LEFT TO RIGHT) STRIPES
- Yes
- No

REQUEST ENTRY TO A PORT

FLAG HAS TWO STRIPES
- Yes
- No

I WISH TO COMMUNICATE WITH YOU

I AM TURNING TO THE RIGHT

YES

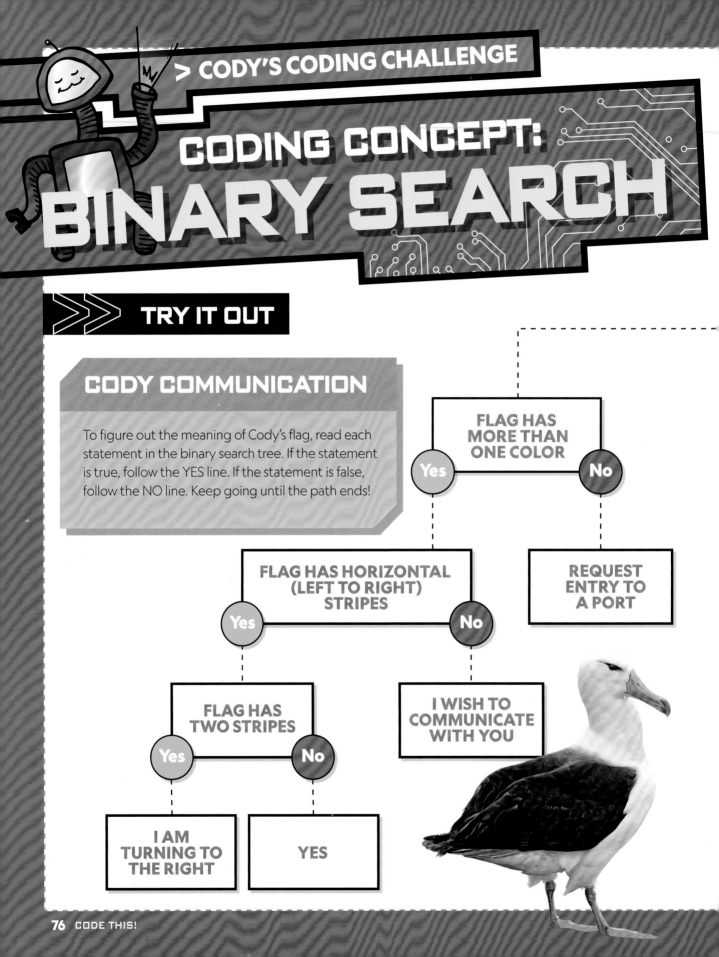

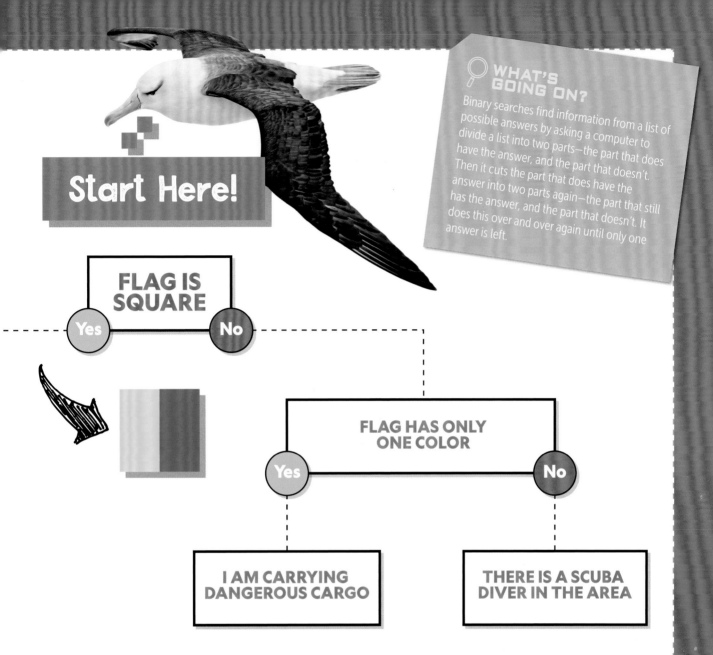

Start Here!

WHAT'S GOING ON?

Binary searches find information from a list of possible answers by asking a computer to divide a list into two parts—the part that does have the answer, and the part that doesn't. Then it cuts the part that does have the answer into two parts again—the part that still has the answer, and the part that doesn't. It does this over and over again until only one answer is left.

FLAG IS SQUARE

Yes No

FLAG HAS ONLY ONE COLOR

Yes No

I AM CARRYING DANGEROUS CARGO

THERE IS A SCUBA DIVER IN THE AREA

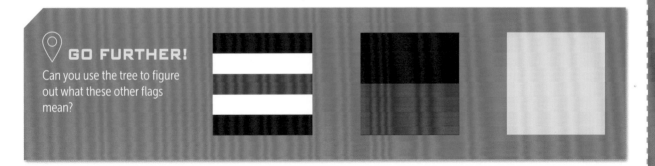

GO FURTHER!

Can you use the tree to figure out what these other flags mean?

BINARY SEARCH CONTINUES ≫

CODING CONCEPT:
BINARY SEARCH

>> TRY IT OUT

TWENTY QUESTIONS

Finding answers doesn't always have to be complicated—you can find out a lot of information by only asking yes and no questions! Try this game to see how, and to discover how a computer binary search works.

> Is it bigger than a refrigerator?

WHAT YOU'LL NEED

- Paper and a pencil
- One friend ... or more

WHAT TO DO

1 One person should think of an object ... but not tell anyone! This person is the **ANSWERER.**

2 The other person (or people) now try to figure out the identity of the mystery object—these people are the **ASKERS.**

3 Each asker takes a turn asking a question about the mystery object. The question must have one of two possible answers: Yes or No. The askers can only ask 20 questions total.

4 Write down each question and its answer on a piece of paper.

5 If one of the askers guesses the mystery object, they get to become the next answerer!

6 If no one can guess the identity of the mystery object, the answerer thinks of a new mystery object.

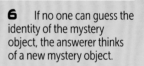

Start here

IS IT LIVING?

Yes   No

IS IT AN ANIMAL?

Yes   No

DOES IT HAVE FUR?

Yes   No

GO FURTHER!

This game is a little like binary search code because the answer to each question eliminates some possible objects. For example, if the answer to "Is it alive?" is "No," then the askers know that the mystery object isn't an animal.

Go back to each question and write down some of the objects that were eliminated after the answer to each question.

DEEP-SEA SURPRISES

OBJECTIVE: WRITE AN ALGORITHM FOR CODY TO PHOTOGRAPH EACH CREATURE AND SEND ITS NAME TO THE EXPLORERS.

ANGLER FISH

SPIDER CRAB

VAMPIRE SQUID

TUBE WORM

OK, Coder Crew. You've learned a lot in this chapter about debugging, binary searches, and binary code. Time to put it all together and send Cody on a deep-sea expedition.

Cody's mission is to **find and photograph each deep-sea creature** shown on the map. Cody needs to first **get to the creature without going through the dark spots.** Then Cody should **snap a photo** of the creature. Finally, Cody should **send the Explorers back on the ship the creature's name using ASCII code.** Then Cody can move on to the next creature.

Write your algorithm for Cody to find and photograph each sea creature and send its name back to the Explorers. Then follow your algorithm below. Don't forget to debug your code.

Hints: When you're debugging, don't forget to check each line—there might be more than one mistake!

Don't forget to stack the letters of each critter's name. Computers read ASCII code top to bottom.

>> 3 >>

CHAPTER 3
SAVE THE SATELLITE

CODING CONCEPTS IN THIS CHAPTER:

| TRIAL AND ERROR | USERS AND EVENTS | PIXELS | DECOMPOSITION |

THE CHALLENGE

>> BROKEN SATELLITE

OBJECTIVE: PROGRAM CODY TO FIX A SATELLITE SO THE EXPLORERS CAN CHECK OUT AN ERUPTING VOLCANO ON ONE OF JUPITER'S MOONS.

>> THE SITUATION

There are **volcanoes all over space.** Some, like the ones on Earth, spew lava. Others, called **cryovolcanoes,** spew supercold liquids. **Jupiter's moon Io** is one of the most volcanically active worlds in our solar system. And the Explorers think one of its active volcanoes is erupting! But the satellite that sends images back from space is not functioning properly. Can you help Cody take the right steps to get the satellite working again?

WHEN YOU'RE PROGRAMMING ONE COMPUTER TO TALK TO ANOTHER COMPUTER, DIRECTIONS NEED TO BE EXTRA CLEAR!

THE BROKEN SATELLITE IS HOLDING UP RESEARCH, SO THE FASTER YOUR PROGRAMS CAN RUN, THE FASTER IT'S BACK IN ACTION.
Hmmm ... something's not right.

CODING CONCEPT: TRIAL AND ERROR

DECODE THE CONCEPT

Have you ever heard the phrase "We all make mistakes"? Well, it's true! But one of the most important ways we learn is through **trial and error.** Trial and error works like this:

1. Try a solution

2. Fail

3. Go back to **step 1** until you succeed.

Trial and error can be frustrating, but learning how *not* to do something is as important as learning how to do it. That way, you can save time by not making the same mistakes you've already made. Coders learn a lot through trial and error.

If at first you can't ride a turtle, try, try again!

MAGIC SQUARES:

Magic Squares may not be magic, but they are the subject of magical stories. According to one ancient legend from China, a turtle with a Magic Square on its shell was able to help keep a river from flooding!

THE MAGIC SQUARE PUZZLE

Solving Magic Square puzzles usually requires a little bit of trial and error. To solve a Magic Square puzzle, you need to follow two rules:

1. You can only use the numbers 1 through 9, and you can only use each number one time.

2. The sum of the numbers in each column, row, and diagonal must be the same.

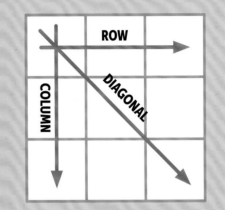

Copy this magic square onto a piece of paper to try it for yourself.

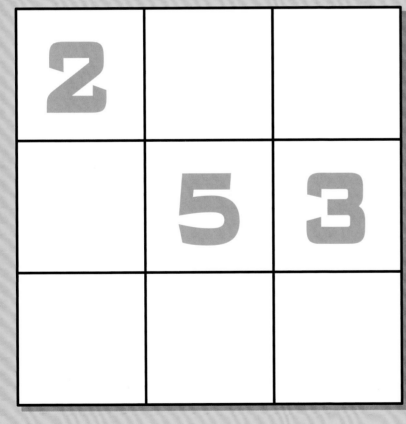

THINK ABOUT IT

How would your strategy change if you knew the number that all the rows, columns, and diagonals added up to in the Magic Square before you started to solve the problem?

WHAT'S GOING ON?

Magic Squares aren't magic at all, of course—they're based on math. The math is based on the number of rows and columns in the square. Completing the square can take a lot of trial and error. One column and row might add up right, but that doesn't mean they all will.

CODING CONCEPT: USERS & EVENTS

DECODE THE CONCEPT

As a computer's **user,** you are able to control what the computer does. Any time you click a mouse or touch a key on the keyboard, you create an **event.** A program on the computer picks up on the event. What happens next depends on the code!

When writing code, a coder needs to think not only about what the code will do, but also what will trigger that event.

TAKE A CODE THAT LOOKS LIKE THIS:

```
JUMP
```

The coder connects that command block to something the user can control. For example:

```
WHEN SPACE BAR
JUMP
```

If our frogbot reads this code, it will jump in place when the user presses the space bar.

THE MAIN EVENT

Using the command blocks in the toolbox, pair the codes to make frogbot respond to the user pressing the arrow keys.

CODE TOOLBOX

WHEN LEFT ARROW

WHEN RIGHT ARROW

WHEN UP ARROW

WHEN DOWN ARROW

JUMP LEFT

JUMP RIGHT

JUMP UP

LAND

💡 THINK ABOUT IT

What would happen if you connected a move-left command to the right-arrow key?

> YOUR TURN

CODING CONCEPT: USERS & EVENTS

>> TRY IT OUT

YOU BE THE VIDEO GAME CHARACTER

Video games are all about users and events. Think about it—if you, the player, didn't have to do something to make something happen in the game, well, it wouldn't be much of a challenge, would it? The trick is to make each event happen at just the right time. That can be tricky, but it's also the fun of mastering the game. Grab a friend and see if you can become user/event champs.

WHAT YOU'LL NEED

- A balloon
- A long piece of string or yarn
- Tape
- A friend
- Pieces of paper and markers

WHAT TO DO

1 BLOW UP THE BALLOON AND KNOT IT. Tie the string to one end of the balloon.

2 Ask an adult to help you **TIE OR TAPE THE STRING TO THE CEILING** in the middle of the room. The balloon should hang high enough so that both you and your friend have to jump to touch it (but not so high that you can't reach it at all).

3 WRITE EACH OF THE SYMBOLS IN THE TOOLBOX ON A SEPARATE PIECE OF PAPER. Make sure the symbols are large enough to be seen from across the room. These represent keys on a keyboard.

1, 2

3

CODING CONNECTION

Event commands are what make video games so much fun. Some event commands are linked to keys or the mouse, but others occur because of other parts of code. The clinking sound made when you pick up a coin or the springy boing sound made when a character jumps are the result of event commands.

CODE TOOLBOX

< Move one step left
> Move one step right
∧ Move one step forward
SPACE Jump

VIDEO GAME CHARACTER CONTINUES ≫≫

WHAT TO DO

4   HAVE ONE PERSON STAND DIRECTLY ACROSS FROM THE OTHER PERSON on the opposite side of the room.

5   ONE PERSON WILL HAVE ALL OF THE SYMBOLS. This person is the **user**. The other person will follow what the symbols say. This person is the video game **character**.

6   THE USER HOLDS UP A SYMBOL. The character then does the action represented by the symbol.

7   THE GOAL OF THE GAME is to have the video game character jump up and touch the balloon.

4, 5, 6

Did some bunny say video games?

CODE TOOLBOX

< Move one step left
> Move one step right
^ Move one step forward
SPACE Jump

TENNIS FOR TWO

One of the earliest video games dates back to 1958. Players of the game Tennis for Two tried to hit an electronic "ball" back and forth over a net. Users could only do one of two things: twist a knob to control the angle of the ball or press a button to "hit" the ball back to the other side.

THINK ABOUT IT

What other keys and events could you add to the balloon game?

CODING CONCEPT:
USERS & EVENTS

>> ## TRY IT OUT

CODE TOOLBOX

REMOTE-CONTROL CODY

The first thing that Cody needs to do to get the satellite back up and running is to push some of the buttons on the control panel. Use the command blocks to write a code that will tell Cody what to do when the Explorers press keyboard buttons back on Earth. Write out the whole algorithm for the Explorers and Cody to press the buttons in the right order. The satellite should move every time Cody presses a button.

- WHEN LEFT ARROW
- WHEN RIGHT ARROW
- WHEN UP ARROW
- WHEN DOWN ARROW
- WHEN SPACE BAR
- WHEN PUSH BUTTON
- MOVE LEFT
- MOVE RIGHT
- MOVE UP
- MOVE DOWN
- PUSH BUTTON
- REPEAT ● TIMES
- DO
- SATELLITE MOVES

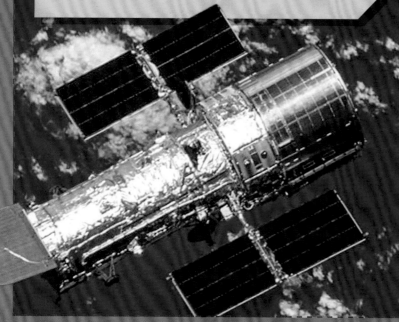

CODING CONCEPT: PIXELS

Just call me Spot!

DECODE THE CONCEPT

All the images, or **graphics,** on a computer screen are made of **pixels.** Coders tell which of these dots should be colored in by using code. Let's say a coder wanted to create this picture on the screen.

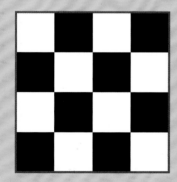

How can you write code for the pattern shown?

PIXEL

The word "pixel" was made by combining parts of two other words: **"pict"** from picture, and **"el"** from element.

Here's how it works.

1. Start in the first space of the grid, the one that's in the upper left-hand corner. (Don't start outside the grid!)

START

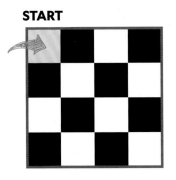

2. The first space is white, so you can just write code to move one space to the right: **>**

This space is black, so you need to use a command that means "color this space in!": **X**

3. Move right to the next space: **>**

It's white, so move right again: **>** and then tell the computer to color the space in: **X**

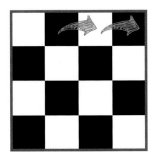

4. Oops, out of squares! Tell the computer to move down one space: **D**

5. That space is white, so tell the computer to move one space to the left: **<**

It's a black space! So color it in: **X**

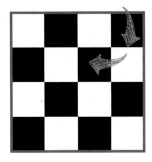

6. Move over two spaces to get to the next black square: **< <** and color it in: **X**

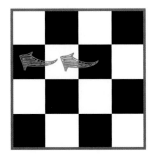

THE CODE FOR THE FIRST TWO ROWS OF THE CHECKERBOARD LOOKS LIKE THIS:

>X>>XD<X<<X

CAN YOU FINISH THE REST?

> YOUR TURN

CODING CONCEPT: PIXELS

WHAT YOU'LL NEED

- Graph paper and a plain piece of paper
- Markers, pens, or pencils
- A friend

>> TRY IT OUT

PIXEL PAINTING

Most early computers were only able to make pictures and words out of two colors. Today, many computer monitors can display over 16 million shades and colors!

Can you correctly write code for a pixel picture like the one on the next page?

You can make pictures out of dots? Color me impressed!

WHAT TO DO

1 Starting in the upper left-hand corner, and moving to the right and then down, **SEE WHICH PIXELS SHOULD BE COLORED IN.**

2 Now **WRITE YOUR CODE.** Using the symbols in the toolbox, write code that your friend can use to re-create the hippo on the graph paper.

3 When you have finished, **ASK A FRIEND TO FOLLOW YOUR CODE** using a clean piece of graph paper. Does the picture look exactly the same as the original?

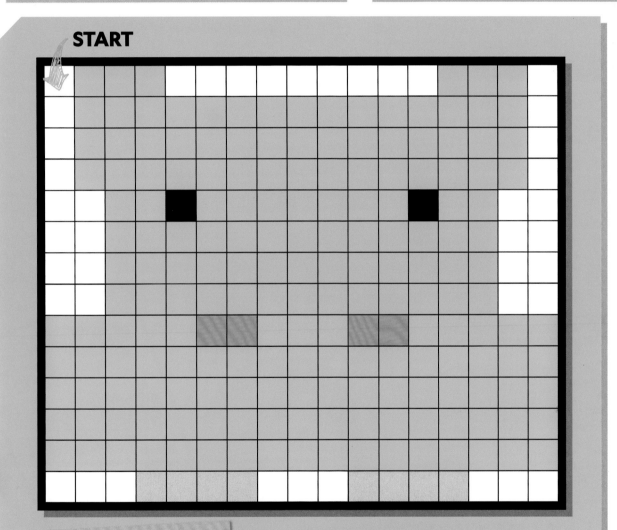

CODE TOOLBOX

> Move right
< Move left
D Move down
X Color in black

B Color in blue
P Color in pink
G Color in gray

START

THINK ABOUT IT

Can you draw your own design or picture on a piece of graph paper, and then write code for it?

WHAT'S GOING ON?

All the things we see on a computer screen, from the words we type to the moving graphics in our favorite games, are there because of the way code tells a computer to light up pixels on a computer screen.

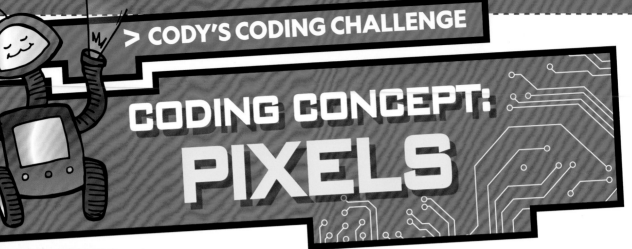

CODING CONCEPT: PIXELS

TRY IT OUT

WHICH BUTTON?

The next step to fixing the satellite is for Cody to push four buttons on the dashboard. The Explorers need to tell Cody what it should be looking for. The button code has to be an exact match of what's in Cody's robot memory, or it won't know which buttons to push. (It's fussy like that.) Cody can't read the picture, so you need to send it clear directions of what each button looks like. Can you write the code for each of these pictures? Then Cody will know what buttons to look for.

CODE TOOLBOX

> Move right
< Move left
M Move down
X Color in black
R Color in red
Y Color in yellow
P Color in pink
G Color in gray
T Color in tan
B Color in blue
L Color in light green
D Color in dark green

BUTTON 1

START

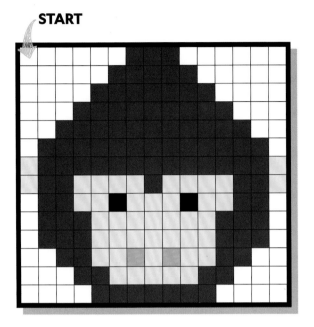

BUTTON 2

START

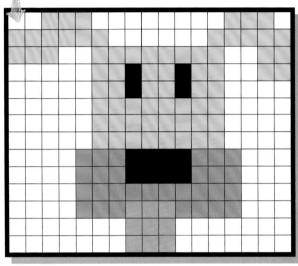

BUTTON 3

START

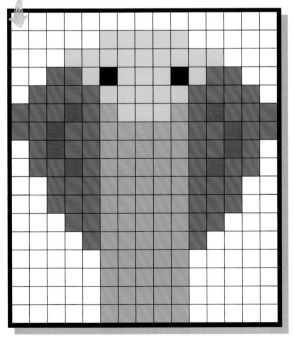

BUTTON 4

START

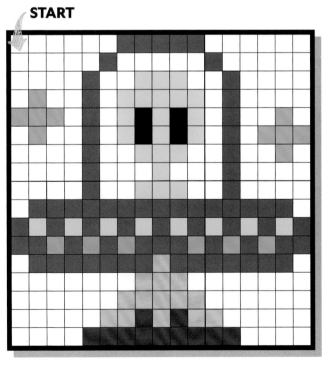

CODING CONCEPT: DECOMPOSITION

DECODE THE CONCEPT

Sometimes problems can feel pretty big. And it's no different for coders when they're writing algorithms. **Decomposition** is one strategy that can help make big problems easier to deal with. In decomposition, you break a big problem down into smaller pieces.

? DID YOU KNOW?

Musicians like Mozart and Beethoven are called composers—they put together small things (like notes) in the right order to make something bigger—like a symphony. Decomposition of a problem is the opposite—it's breaking down something big into smaller pieces.

I can sleep all day long by breaking up the day into 2-hour nap blocks!

DISC DECOMPOSITION

One of the ways to practice decomposition is to use a puzzle that looks like this.

The goal of this puzzle is to move all the discs from Tower 1 to Tower 3. There are two constraints: You cannot put a larger disc onto a smaller disc, and you must move only one disc at a time.

Try making some discs of your own to see if you can decompose a solution to the problem.

WHAT YOU'LL NEED

- Construction paper
- This pattern:

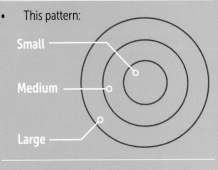

Small

Medium

Large

- A pen or pencil
- Scissors
- A piece of blank paper

WHAT TO DO

1 **DRAW EACH CIRCLE** on a separate piece of construction paper.

2 Carefully **CUT OUT EACH CIRCLE** with the scissors.

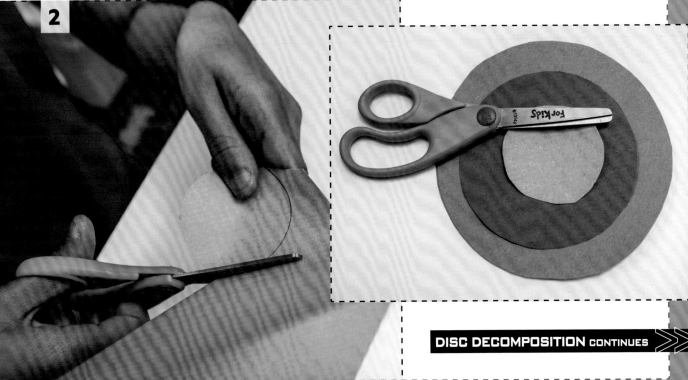

DISC DECOMPOSITION CONTINUES >>

DISC DECOMPOSITION

Did someone say discs? I'll play!

WHAT TO DO

3 DIVIDE THE PLAIN PIECE OF PAPER INTO THREE COLUMNS. Label the first column "Tower 1," the second column "Tower 2," and the third column "Tower 3."

4 PLACE THE THREE CIRCLES IN A STACK IN THE COLUMN LABELED TOWER 1. The largest circle should be on the bottom, and the smallest one on top.

5 Can you figure out how to **MOVE ALL THE DISCS TO TOWER 3** without ever putting a larger disc on top of a smaller one?

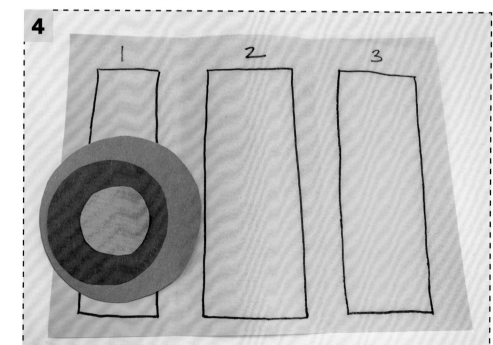

5

WHAT'S GOING ON?

Solving problems can be a big challenge. So coders break them into small pieces ... and smaller pieces ... and even smaller pieces, until they find a piece of the problem that they can solve. Then they apply what they've learned to solve other pieces of the problem. They repeat this process until they can put all their little solutions together to solve the entire problem!

THINK ABOUT IT

Can you write an algorithm that someone else could use to solve this problem?

DID YOU KNOW?

This puzzle gets harder as you add more discs to the stack. There is a legend in which people were trying to solve this problem using 64 discs. If the legend happened in real life, the puzzle would take 585 billion years to finish!

CODING CONCEPT: DECOMPOSITION

>> TRY IT OUT

MIRROR MOVING

The last step Cody has to do is to move these telescope mirrors from post A to post C. Cody needs to be very careful. The mirrors are fragile. So Cody can only move one at a time, and a smaller mirror can't have a larger one on top of it. Write an algorithm for Cody to use.

Post A

Post B

Post C

SAVE THE SATELLITE

OK, Coder Crew. You've learned a lot in this chapter about **trial and error, adding user events, pixels,** and **decomposition.** It's time to put it all together ... and save the satellite! You'll need to send these instructions to tell Cody which buttons need to be pushed, and in what order. Can you write code to send this picture to Cody?

BUTTON ORDER

START

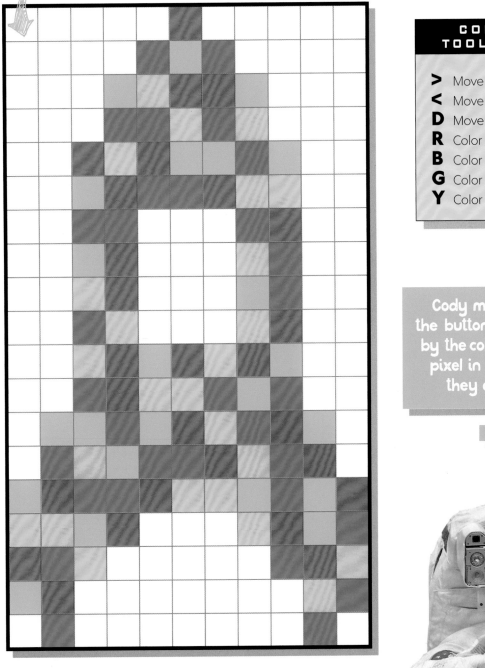

CODE TOOLBOX

> **>** Move right
> **<** Move left
> **D** Move down
> **R** Color in blue
> **B** Color in blue
> **G** Color in green
> **Y** Color in yellow

Cody must press the buttons indicated by the color of each pixel in the order they appear.

CHAPTER 4

TRICKY TEPUI

CODING CONCEPTS IN THIS CHAPTER:

OPTIMIZATION   MAKING SHAPES   CONDITIONALS

THE CHALLENGE

OBJECTIVE: PROGRAM CODY TO GET A PHOTO OF A JAGUAR.

THE SITUATION

Tepuis are South American plateaus—rocky islands that rise high above the rain forests of **Venezuela.** Some tepui are shrouded in swirling clouds and mist all year long, making any expeditions to them extremely treacherous. But tepui are also home to some of the world's coolest big cats, including the jaguar and the **puma.** Can you help the Explorers by programming Cody to snap a shot of one of these amazing animals?

CODING CONCEPT: OPTIMIZATION

DECODING THE CONCEPT

If you've ever had to pack a bag for a long trip, you know that you can't take it all. You have to make some tough choices about what to bring, and what to leave behind. To do that, you have to ... that's right ... **optimize** the space in your bag by choosing the things you need most that will fit into your bag.

It's the same with coding. Though there are often many ways to write the same directions, shorter code will make the computer run more efficiently.

TRY OPTIMIZING THE BEST COMBINATION OF THINGS ON THIS PAGE. CAN YOU MAKE THE BEST CHOICES FOR A TRIP TO THE BEACH?

CODY'S CAMP CHAIR

Jaguars are notoriously shy animals, so it might be some time before one feels safe enough to approach Cody's camp. Cody needs to be prepared to wait a while. **Can you construct a model of a chair** that's light and easy to fold up (so it can fit inside Cody's cargo compartment) but sturdy enough to hold Cody's weight?

WHAT YOU'LL NEED

- Paper and pencil
- A sandwich bag
- A potato or apple (to represent Cody)
- Scissors
- Tape
- Toothpicks
- Wooden craft sticks
- Plastic wrap
- Aluminum foil
- A piece of cloth about 5 inches (13 cm) square

WHAT TO DO

1 USE THE PIECE OF PAPER AND PENCIL TO SKETCH A FEW IDEAS FOR YOUR CHAIR. Your model should be small enough to fit into the plastic baggie. (You can fold your chair up or take it apart, as long as you can put it back together when you "get" to the camp.) Remember: You can only use the materials you have on the list!

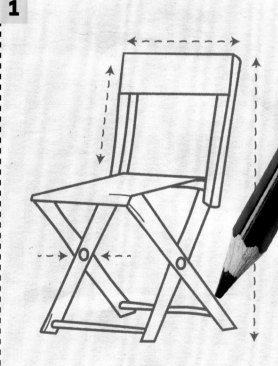

1

CODY'S CAMP CHAIR CONTINUES

CODY'S CAMP CHAIR

WHAT TO DO

2 Once you have two (or more!) ideas, **PICK YOUR FAVORITE,** and build it.

3 **MAKE SURE YOU TEST YOUR MODEL CHAIR**—does it fit into the baggie? Does it hold your model Cody? If not, try another design.

CODING CONNECTION

When coders write a computer program, they have to make some of the same kinds of choices you do when finding a solution to a problem. Some kinds of code won't work with one another or will make the program run slowly. Coders have to think about the goal of the program and then choose the best, or optimal, code that works.

THINK ABOUT IT

How would your solution change if the size of the bag was changed? How about if you used an egg or a bigger potato or apple to represent Cody?

GO FURTHER!

Can you build a better model chair using other materials you can find around the house?

> CODY'S CODING CHALLENGE

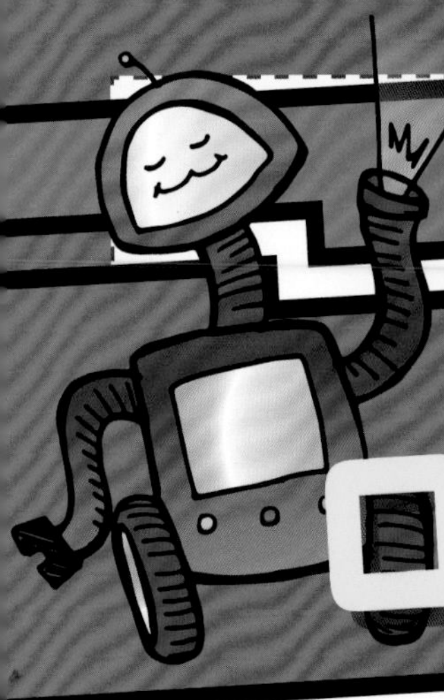

CODING CONCEPT: OPTIMIZATION

TRY IT OUT

CODY'S BACKPACK

It's a big climb to the top of the tepui! Cody doesn't have much room in its backpack, and it can carry only 15 pounds (6.8 kg). **Which things should Cody take on the journey?**

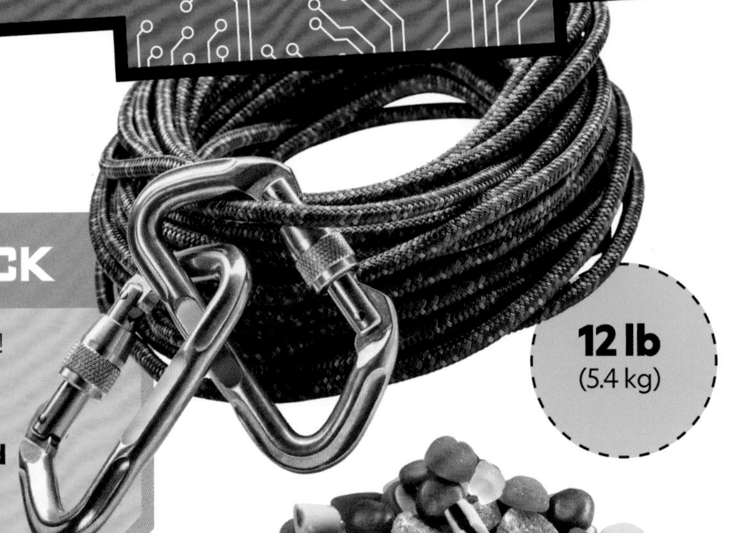

12 lb
(5.4 kg)

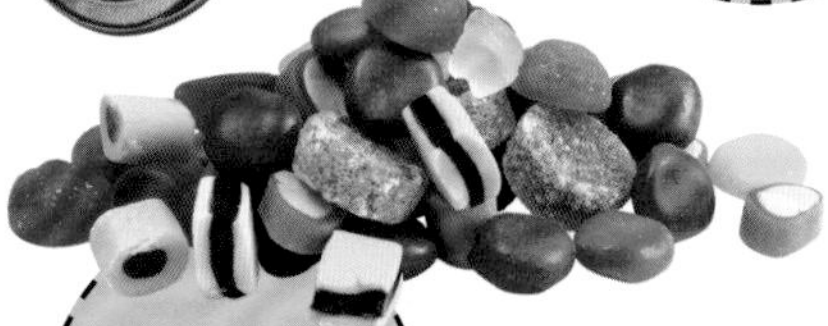

5 lb
(2.2 kg)

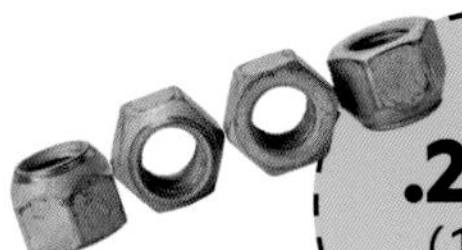

.25 lb
(.11 kg)

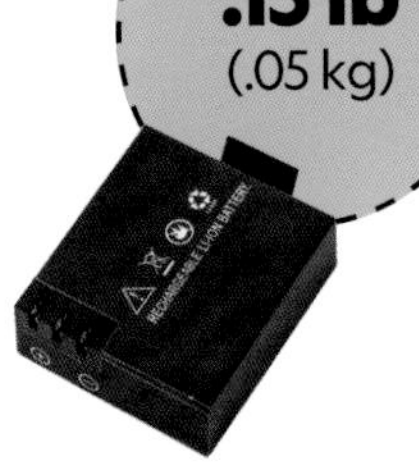

.13 lb
(.05 kg)

Hint: Don't forget the goal of the journey—get a photo of a jaguar!

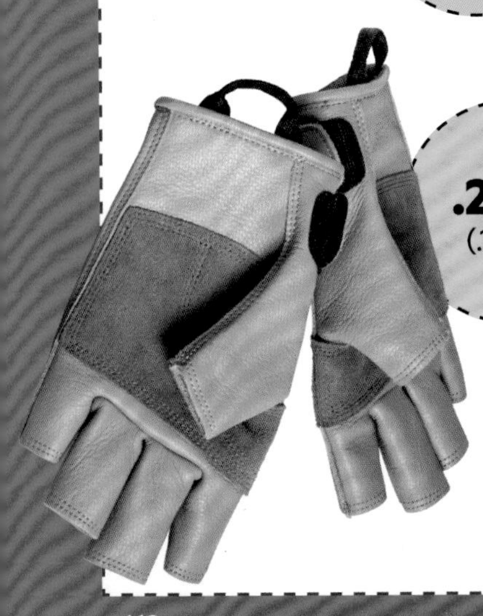

.25 lb
(.11 kg)

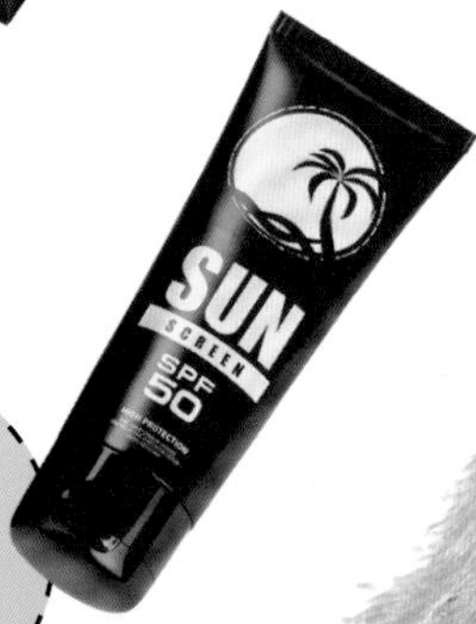

.13 lb
(.05 kg)

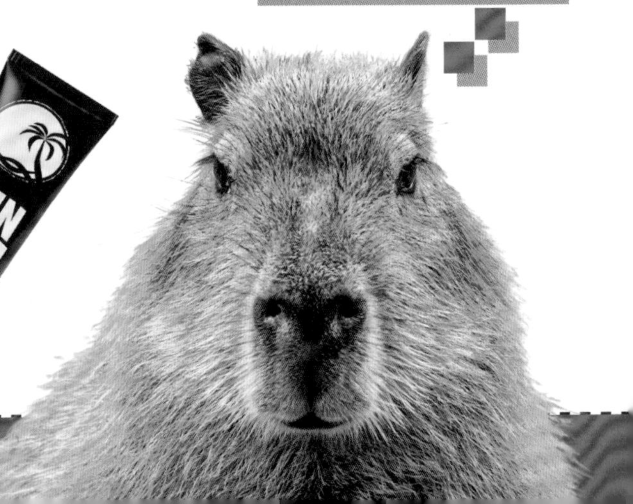

.13 lb
(.06 kg)

.34 lb
(.15 kg)

1 lb
(.45 kg)

5 lb
(2.2 kg)

0.5 lb
(.22 kg)

.63 lb
(.28 kg)

0.3 lb
(.14 kg)

2 lb
(0.9 kg)

THE KNAPSACK PROBLEM

One famous optimization problem is called the Knapsack Problem. The goal of this problem is to be able to carry as many valuable things as possible without going over a limit.

CODING CONCEPT: MAKING SHAPES

DECODING THE CONCEPT

Shapes are probably one of the first things that you learned how to draw. Simple shapes—like circles, squares, and triangles—are the basics that even professional artists and graphic designers use to create all kinds of drawings.

It's the same with coding, too. Student computer programmers don't start by writing graphics code for a super-realistic 3D video game. Instead, they learn to give computers directions on how to draw those same simple shapes they first made themselves. And they don't get to see their computer drawings until they run the program.

I'm totally in shape.

>> TRY IT OUT

SHAPING UP

Simple geometric shapes are easy to draw—and they're supposed to be! Drawing objects with basic shapes can help communicate an idea quickly and easily. Grab a friend and try this shape-drawing challenge.

WHAT YOU'LL NEED

- Pencil and paper
- A friend

1

2

WHAT TO DO

1 CHOOSE A SHAPE OR DRAWING FROM THE ONES SHOWN. Or, choose something from your imagination!

2 CLOSE YOUR EYES, AND DRAW THE PICTURE. How close did you come to the original?

3 CHOOSE ANOTHER PIC-TURE. This time, ask someone else to give you directions on how to draw the picture after your close your eyes. Move your pencil exactly how they tell you—and no peeking!

3

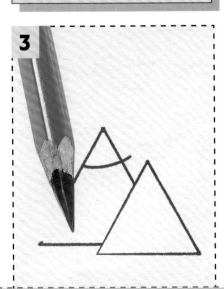

🔍 WHAT'S GOING ON?

Remember that programmers can't just tell a computer to draw something. They have to write directions that tell the computer exactly how to make a shape—and they don't know for sure what the shape looks like until they run the program. It's a little bit like drawing with your eyes closed!

💡 THINK ABOUT IT

Which shapes are hardest to draw? Why? Try one of the shapes again. How can you change the directions to make them better?

GO FURTHER!

Give a friend directions on how to draw something without telling him or her what it is!

CODING CONCEPT:
MAKING SHAPES

>> TRY IT OUT

PROGRAMMING THE ARTIST

Are you ready to improve your graphics programming skills? Think like a programmer by using command blocks to write an algorithm.

CODE TOOLBOX

MOVE FORWARD 12 INCHES (31 CM)

TURN LEFT

TURN RIGHT

REPEAT ● TIMES

DO

MAKE A DOT ON THE GROUND

WHAT YOU'LL NEED

- Masking tape (for an inside activity) or chalk (for outside)

- Coins (for an inside activity)

- Pencil and paper

- Yardstick (or meterstick)

No llama drama here! It's hip to be a square.

WHAT TO DO

1 FIND AN OPEN SPOT, either inside (such as on an empty dining table) or outside (such as the sidewalk) that's about 3 feet (1 m) square.

2 MAKE A SMALL MARK TO SYMBOLIZE YOUR BEGINNING SPOT using either masking tape (if you're inside) or chalk (if you're outside).

3 Using the commands in the toolbox above, **WRITE AN ALGORITHM THAT WILL MAKE A SQUARE** that has sides that are 3 feet (1 m) in length.

4 TRY IT OUT! Does your code successfully make the square?

THINK ABOUT IT

If you added the command blocks "Turn halfway to the right" and "Turn halfway to the left" could you ...

... write the code for a triangle?

... write the code that would make the first letter of your name?

WHAT'S GOING ON?

The images we see when we use our favorite apps or play our favorite video games all are based on code. The code instructs the computer on how to color and shade each pixel on the screen. The more complex the image, the more commands in the code!

MOTION CAPTURE

Some computer graphics get a little bit of help from real live actors. The graphics in many video games and some movies start with an actor in a special suit. Special computer parts sense the movements of the actor inside the suit. Then people use graphics programs to create the video game or movie character.

CODING CONCEPT: MAKING SHAPES

>> TRY IT OUT

SETTING UP THE PICTURE

The Nat Geo Explorers want to get a picture of a jaguar. To do this, they have to make sure the jaguar is in a certain spot. They'll need Cody to trace a rectangle on the ground that will fit into the camera's viewer. **Using the command blocks, write an algorithm** to help Cody use its special marker to mark the area for the picture.

CODE TOOLBOX

MOVE FORWARD 12 INCHES (31 CM)

TURN LEFT

TURN RIGHT

REPEAT ● TIMES

DO

MAKE A DOT ON THE GROUND

CODING CONCEPT: CONDITIONALS

DECODING THE CONCEPT

From the time you wake up in the morning until you go to bed at night, you make decisions—lots of them. Computers can't decide on their own, but they can make choices with the right kind of code. **Conditionals** are special instructions that help computers make decisions.

Conditionals are set up as If/Then statements: If something happens, then do something. For example, if the traffic light is red, then stop. If the condition isn't met (for example, the traffic light is any color but red), then the action won't happen.

IF it's cheese ...

THEN eat the cheese!

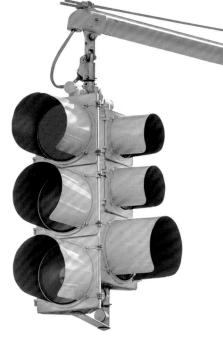

Conditionals can also be set up to give the computer specific instructions about what to do if the condition is met and what to do if it isn't. For a continuous carousel of photos (where the buffalo displays after the fish, for example), that could look something like this:

IF the up arrow is clicked, **THEN** display the photo. **ELSE** wait 3 seconds, then display the next photo to the right.

Can you figure out what that means? What happens if the arrow is clicked? What happens if the arrow isn't clicked?

How would you write a conditional statement to open the photo of the frog?

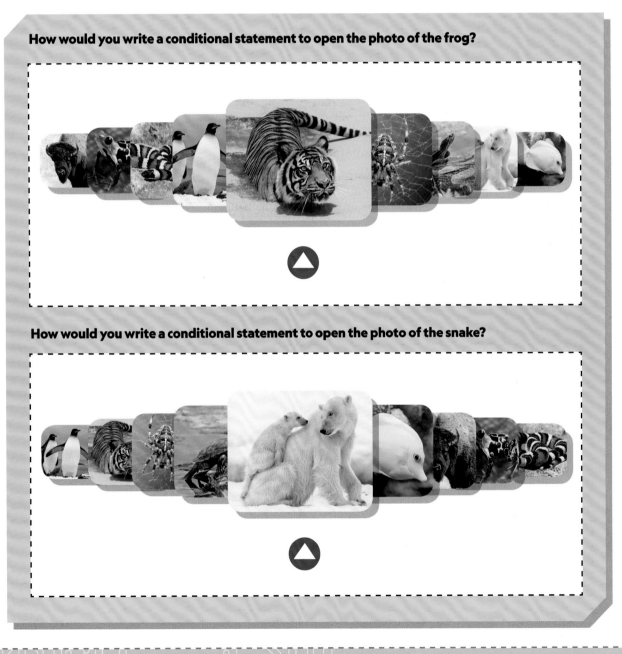

How would you write a conditional statement to open the photo of the snake?

CODING CONCEPT: CONDITIONALS

DECODE THE CONCEPT

Now that you understand how conditionals work, it's time to get coding!

If/Else blocks look like this:

IF you have a nut, THEN give it to me!

IF   THEN

ELSE

To use an If/Else block, just **"plug in"** the right words to describe what condition you want the computer to look for.

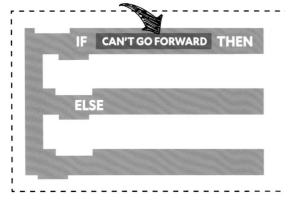

Next **add what the action should be if the condition is true.** For example, if Cody CAN'T GO FORWARD, then it should TURN LEFT.

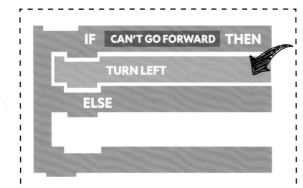

Finally, **add the action that should happen if the condition isn't true.** For example, if Cody *can* go forward, then Cody should MOVE FORWARD 1.

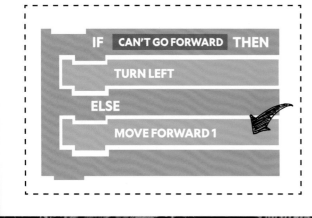

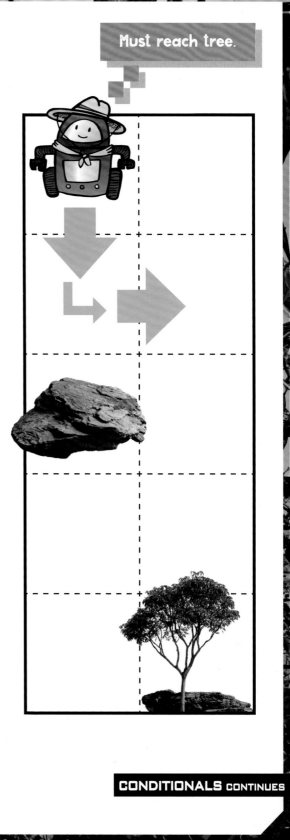

Must reach tree.

CONDITIONALS CONTINUES »

> YOUR TURN

CODING CONCEPT:
CONDITIONALS

>> TRY IT OUT

WHAT YOU'LL NEED

- The game board shown on the following pages
- A die
- A coin or other marker for each person playing
- A few friends to play with

CONDITIONAL LAND

Conditionals are also part of lots of games. Think about it: How many games have you played that rely on something happening or not happening? Many games depend on the number you roll, or the card you draw.

I'm the programmer.

Spots are a condition for being dice ... or a tapir.

Grab a few friends. **It's time to play Conditional Land!**

WHAT TO DO

1 During each round, **ONE PLAYER WILL BE THE PROGRAMMER. EVERYONE ELSE WILL BE COMPUTERS** for that round.

2 To start each round, **THE PROGRAMMER ROLLS THE DIE.** Whatever number comes up on the die will be the IF number for that round.

3 **THE PROGRAMMER DECIDES WHAT ACTION THE COMPUTERS SHOULD DO** whenever they roll the IF number on the die. (See the suggestions if you get stuck!)

4 **EACH COMPUTER WILL TAKE A TURN AND ROLL THE DIE.** If a computer rolls the IF number, he or she will do the action that the programmer chose at the beginning of the round. If they do not roll the IF number, they take the ELSE path, and move the number of spaces on the die forward on the path.

5 **ONCE ALL OF THE COMPUTERS HAVE ROLLED, THE ROUND ENDS.** The person to the right of the programmer becomes the next programmer, and a new round starts.

6 **THE GAME ENDS WHEN SOMEONE REACHES THE END OF THE PATH!**

If there's a game going on, then I'm ready to play!

CONDITIONAL LAND CONTINUES

START

CONDITIONAL
LAND

END

WHAT'S GOING ON?

Conditionals work in computers the same way that binary codes and searches work. There are only two choices: what to do If something happens, or if something doesn't happen. Each time a conditional is written into code, it tells the computer to choose one of two paths. Conditionals can make a lot of things happen. For example, in a video game, IF you press the jump key at the right time, the game continues ... ELSE ... it's Game Over!

THINK ABOUT IT

Can you write an algorithm for a conditional game that uses a coin flip?

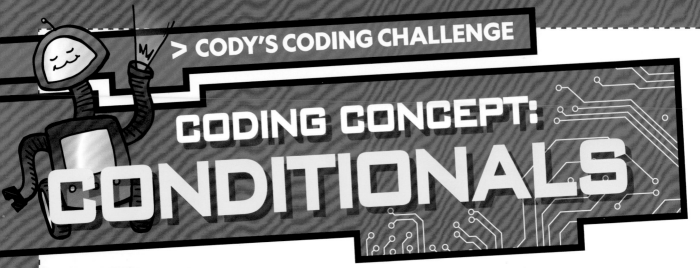

CODING CONCEPT: CONDITIONALS

TRY IT OUT

GETTING HOME

It's time to get Cody home. That might sound easy, but Cody has some decisions to make along the way. Help Cody get to the edge of the tepui by using the command blocks in the toolbox.

WHAT'S GPS?

Cody's map was made, in part, by people using the global positioning system (or GPS for short). GPS devices use satellites in space to send and receive information about where an object is on Earth. Early on, GPS was only available to a small number of people, such as the military. But now these useful pieces of technology are found in many cars, boats, and cell phones.

Hint: Plan out the path you want Cody to take before you start writing the code.

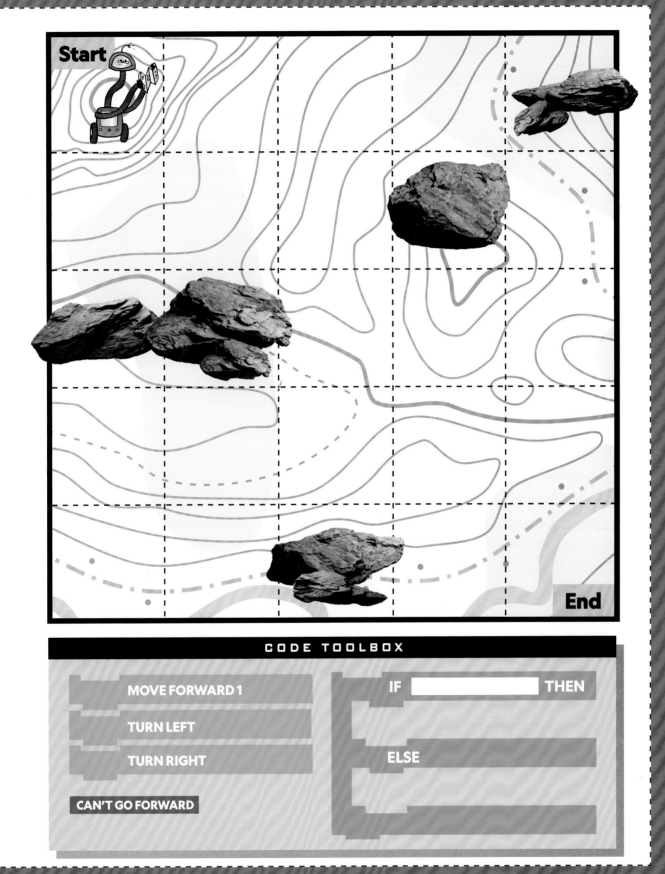

Start

End

CODE TOOLBOX

MOVE FORWARD 1

TURN LEFT

TURN RIGHT

CAN'T GO FORWARD

IF [   ] THEN

ELSE

TRICKY TEPUI

Start

OBJECTIVE: WRITE ALGORITHMS TO HELP CODY SAFELY CLIMB FROM THE TOP OF THE TEPUI DOWN TO BASE CAMP.

OK, Coder Crew. You've learned a lot in this chapter about optimization, making shapes, and conditionals. It's time to put it all together to help Cody pick the best path. Grab a piece of paper and a pencil and **use the command blocks to write algorithms** that will take Cody **down each path.** Then decide which path to send Cody down.

Cheese!

End

CODE TOOLBOX

MOVE FORWARD 1

TURN LEFT

TURN RIGHT

REPEAT ● TIMES

DO

CAN'T GO FORWARD

IF [ ] THEN

ELSE

Start

Start

End

End

AFTERWORD

Computers are powerful machines, but they are still the same as all other machines—they need people to tell them what to do. Algorithms, the instructions that a computer follows to accomplish a task, are written by thinking about how to solve the problem, and then writing the code that helps the computer do it.

Some of the first computers, like ENIAC, took up entire rooms. Today, many people carry a smartphone that can fit in a pocket. The art of computer programming has changed a lot, too. People are inventing new ways to use computers, inventing new types of computers, and figuring out how to make computers run faster and do more than ever before.

But NONE of this would be possible without the thinking power of the human brain. And more important, its curiosity. What can you do? Keep asking questions and keep thinking about problems. After all, programming is just giving a machine some clear directions and the tools to solve problems. What problems will computers solve in the future? The answer could be based on code you might write!

Artificial intelligence computer Watson competes in the TV game show *Jeopardy!* against human opponents.

Roboticists use programming to help robots interact with the real world.

Early computers were the size of an entire room.

This smart technology allows someone to control a "hand" to move a real ball from far away.

SOLUTIONS

CHECK YOUR WORK! Did you come up with these solutions?

One of the best things about coding is that you can make it your own. Just as there's often more than one way to think about a problem, there's often more than one way to write code that works. So, some of the solutions in this section may not be the only ones! You might come up with code that works but doesn't look exactly like our solutions.

CHAPTER 1

PAGE 23 HOW TO MAKE A SMOOTHIE

STEPS:
Peel a banana and break it into pieces.
Put banana pieces into the blender.
Get a cup of your favorite frozen fruit.
Put the fruit into the blender.
Measure out ½ cup of milk or yogurt.
Put the milk or yogurt in the blender.
Put the lid on the blender.
Turn the blender on to its highest setting.
Wait 3 or 4 minutes.
Turn off the blender.
Take the lid off the blender.
Pour the smoothie into a glass.
Drink the smoothie.

PAGES 28-29 TRAVELING EXPLORER

The shortest path would be: groceries, then post office, then the library (or in backward order) for a total of 29 minutes.

PAGE 31 CAVE EXPLORER CODY

The shortest path:

A → B

B → C

C → D

D → A

Total time:
140 minutes

PAGE 33 SECRET CIPHERS

(from top to bottom)

YOU SOLVED THE CIPHER

CODY LOVES EXPLORING

COUNT THE FROGBOTS

PAGE 34 SUBSTITUTION CIPHERS

A GIRAFFE'S TONGUE IS BLACK!
Z FHQZEED'R SNMFTD HR AKZBJ!

BATS HAVE THUMBS!
AZSR GZUD SGTLAR!

PAGE 35 SUBSTITUTION CIPHERS

FNKCEHRG BZM KDZQM
SN CN SQHBJR.
**GOLDFISH CAN LEARN
TO DO TRICKS.**

LZKD ODMFTHMR
JDDO DFFR VZQL.
**MALE PENGUINS KEEP
EGGS WARM.**

AQHFGS BNKNQR VZQM
ZVZX OQDCZSNQR.
**BRIGHT COLORS WARN
AWAY PREDATORS.**

ZM NBSNOTR GZR
SGQDD GDZQSR.
**AN OCTOPUS HAS
THREE HEARTS.**

MN SVN SHFDQR'
RSQHODR ZQD ZKHJD.
**NO TWO TIGERS'
STRIPES ARE ALIKE.**

PAGE 41 CAVE CODES

PDA OPQZU
THE STUDY
KB YWRAO
OF CAVES
EO YWHHAZ
IS CALLED
OLAHAKHKCU
SPELEOLOGY

PAGE 45 MOUSEBOT ON THE MOVE

Our Solution:

Start

∧
∧
∧
>
∧
∧
>
∧
∧
∧
∧
∧
<
<
∧
∧
∧
∧

Stop

PAGE 47 HELP MOUSEBOT REACH THE TOADSTOOL

Our Solution:

REPEAT **5** TIMES
DO ∧

<

REPEAT **4** TIMES
DO ∧

<

REPEAT **3** TIMES
DO ∧

PAGES 48-49 CODY AND THE LABYRINTH

Our Solution:

REPEAT **4** TIMES
DO ∧

<

REPEAT **4** TIMES
DO ∧

>

∧

PAGES 50-51 THE MYSTERIOUS CAVE

REPEAT **3** TIMES
DO ∧

TAKE PHOTO

REPEAT **3** TIMES
DO ∧

TAKE PHOTO

∧
>

REPEAT **5** TIMES
DO ∧

<

REPEAT **2** TIMES
DO ∧

<
∧

TAKE PHOTO

REPEAT **3** TIMES
DO ∧

<

REPEAT **2** TIMES
DO ∧

<

REPEAT **8** TIMES
DO ∧

<

REPEAT **2** TIMES
DO ∧

TAKE PHOTO

REPEAT **2** TIMES
DO ∧

TAKE PHOTO

<

REPEAT **2** TIMES
DO ∧

<

REPEAT **2** TIMES
DO ∧

>

REPEAT **3** TIMES
DO ∧

>

TAKE PHOTO

<

REPEAT **2** TIMES
DO ∧

<
∧
>
∧

TAKE PHOTO

∧
>

REPEAT **9** TIMES
DO ∧

CHAPTER 2

PAGE 59 HOP TO IT!

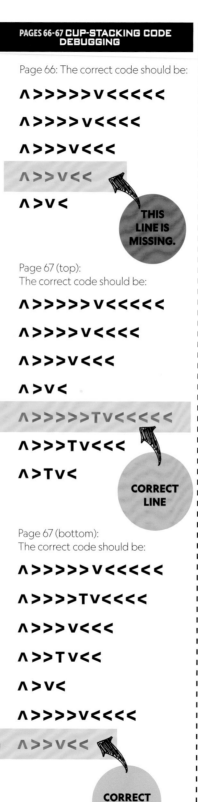

PAGES 60-61 SPECIAL DELIVERY

STEPS:

1 Take the dog to the boat, leaving the cat and picnic basket together on the shore.

2 Leave the dog on the boat, return to the shore alone.

3 Carry the picnic basket to the boat. Leave the picnic basket on the boat, bring the dog back to shore.

4 Leave the dog on the shore, and take the cat to the boat. Leave the cat on the boat with the picnic basket.

5 Return to the shore alone.

6 Pick up the dog and take it to the boat.

PAGES 66-67 CUP-STACKING CODE DEBUGGING

Page 66: The correct code should be:

∧ > > > > > ∨ < < < < <

∧ > > > > ∨ < < < <

∧ > > > ∨ < < <

∧ > > ∨ < <

THIS LINE IS MISSING.

∧ > ∨ <

Page 67 (top):
The correct code should be:

∧ > > > > > ∨ < < < < <

∧ > > > > ∨ < < < <

∧ > > > ∨ < < <

∧ > ∨ <

∧ > > > > > T ∨ < < < < <

CORRECT LINE

∧ > > > T ∨ < < <

∧ > T ∨ <

Page 67 (bottom):
The correct code should be:

∧ > > > > > ∨ < < < < <

∧ > > > > T ∨ < < < <

∧ > > > ∨ < < <

∧ > > T ∨ < <

∧ > ∨ <

∧ > > > > ∨ < < < <

∧ > > ∨ < <

CORRECT LINE

PAGES 68-69 CODY MISSES THE MARK

To get Cody to the camera, add these blocks to the bottom of the code that's already there:

MOVE FORWARD

TURN LEFT

MOVE FORWARD

PAGE 73 ASCII ASSIGNMENT

P
A
N
D
A

PAGE 76-77 CODY COMMUNICATION

The flag means:
I WISH TO COMMUNICATE WITH YOU

PAGE 77 BINARY SEARCH: GO FURTHER

YES

I AM TURNING TO THE RIGHT

REQUEST ENTRY TO A PORT

CHAPTER 3

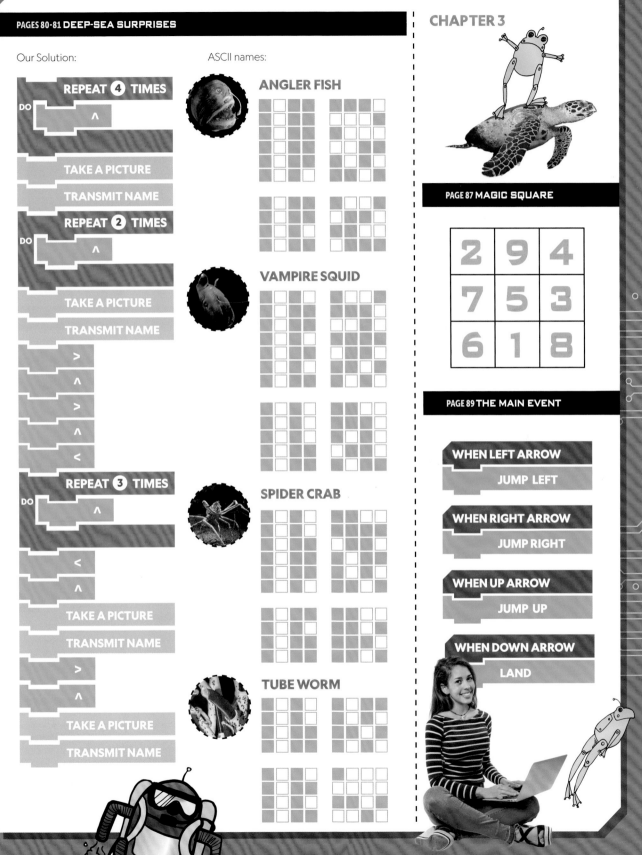

Our Solution:

REPEAT **4** TIMES

DO

Λ

TAKE A PICTURE

TRANSMIT NAME

REPEAT **2** TIMES

DO

Λ

TAKE A PICTURE

TRANSMIT NAME

\>

Λ

\>

Λ

\<

REPEAT **3** TIMES

DO

Λ

\<

Λ

TAKE A PICTURE

TRANSMIT NAME

\>

Λ

TAKE A PICTURE

TRANSMIT NAME

ASCII names:

ANGLER FISH

VAMPIRE SQUID

SPIDER CRAB

TUBE WORM

PAGE 87 MAGIC SQUARE

2	9	4
7	5	3
6	1	8

PAGE 89 THE MAIN EVENT

WHEN LEFT ARROW

JUMP LEFT

WHEN RIGHT ARROW

JUMP RIGHT

WHEN UP ARROW

JUMP UP

WHEN DOWN ARROW

LAND

REPEAT **3** TIMES
DO WHEN UP ARROW
MOVE UP

WHEN LEFT ARROW
MOVE LEFT

WHEN SPACE BAR
PUSH BUTTON

WHEN PUSH BUTTON
SATELLITE MOVES

REPEAT **2** TIMES
DO WHEN DOWN ARROW
MOVE DOWN

WHEN LEFT ARROW
MOVE LEFT

WHEN SPACE BAR
PUSH BUTTON

WHEN PUSH BUTTON
SATELLITE MOVES

WHEN UP ARROW
MOVE UP

WHEN RIGHT ARROW
MOVE RIGHT

WHEN SPACE BAR
PUSH BUTTON

WHEN PUSH BUTTON
SATELLITE MOVES

WHEN LEFT ARROW
MOVE LEFT

WHEN SPACE BAR
PUSH BUTTON

WHEN PUSH BUTTON
SATELLITE MOVES

REPEAT **2** TIMES
DO WHEN RIGHT ARROW
MOVE RIGHT

WHEN DOWN ARROW
MOVE DOWN

WHEN SPACE BAR
PUSH BUTTON

WHEN PUSH BUTTON
SATELLITE MOVES

REPEAT **2** TIMES
DO WHEN UP ARROW
MOVE UP

REPEAT **2** TIMES
DO WHEN LEFT ARROW
MOVE LEFT

WHEN SPACE BAR
PUSH BUTTON

WHEN PUSH BUTTON
SATELLITE MOVES

PAGE 97 PIXELS

The rest of the checkerboard code would be:

`D>X>>XD<X<<X`

PAGES 98-99 PIXEL PAINTING

For pixel puzzles, follow the answers like this:

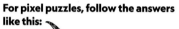

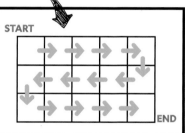

START

END

```
>B>B>B>>>>>>>>>>B>B>B>D
D<B<B<B<B<B<B<B<B<B<B<B<B<B<B<
>B>B>B>B>B>B>B>B>B>B>B>B>B>D
D<B<B<B<B<B<B<B<B<B<B<B<B<B<B<
>>B>B>X>B>B>B>B>B>B>X>B>B>>D
D<<B<B<B<B<B<B<B<B<B<B<B<B<<
>>B>B>B>B>B>B>B>B>B>B>B>B>>D
D<<B<B<B<B<B<B<B<B<B<B<B<B<<
B>B>B>B>B>P>P>B>B>B>P>P>B>B>B>BD
DB<B<B<B<B<B<B<B<B<B<B<B<B<B<B
B>B>B>B>B>B>B>B>B>B>B>B>B>B>BD
DB<B<B<B<B<B<B<B<B<B<B<B<B<B<B
B>B>B>B>B>B>B>B>B>B>B>B>B>B>BD
END<<<G<G<G<G<<<<G<G<G<G<<<
```

PAGES 100-101 WHICH BUTTON?

BUTTON 1
```
>>>>>>G>G>G>>>>>M
M<<<<G<G<G<G<G<G<<<<<
>>>>G>G>G>G>G>G>G>>>>M
M<<<G<G<G<G<G<G<G<G<G<<<
>>G>G>G>G>G>G>G>G>G>G>>M
M<G<G<G<G<G<G<G<G<G<G<G<G<
T>G>G>G>G>G>G>G>G>G>G>G>TM
M>T<G<G<T<T<T<T<G<T<T<T<G<G<T
>G>G>T>T>X>T>T>X>T>T>G>G>M
M<G<G<G<T<T<T<T<T<T<T<G<G<<
>G>G>G>T>T>T>T>T>T>G>G>G>M
M<<G<G<T<T<P<T<P<T<T<G<G<<
>>>G>G>T>T>T>T>T>G>G>>>M
END<<<<G<G<G<G<G<G<G<<<<<
```

BUTTON 2
```
>>Y>Y>Y>>>>>>>>Y>Y>Y>M
MY<Y<Y<Y<Y<Y<<<<<<<Y<Y<Y<Y<Y
Y>Y>Y>>>>Y>Y>Y>Y>Y>Y>>>>Y>YM
M<<<<<<Y<Y<X<Y<X<Y<Y<<<<Y<Y
>>>>>>Y>Y>X>Y>Y>X>Y>Y>>>>M
M<<<<<<Y<Y<Y<Y<Y<Y<Y<Y<<<<
>>>>>Y>Y>Y>Y>Y>Y>Y>Y>>>>>M
M<<<<<Y<Y<Y<Y<Y<Y<Y<Y<<<<
>>>>T>T>T>X>X>X>X>T>T>T>>>M
M<<<<T<T<X<X<X<X<T<T<T<<<
>>>>T>T>T>T>T>T>T>T>T>>>>M
M<<<<T<T<T<P<P<P<T<T<T<T<<
>>>>>>>P>P>P>>>>>>>M
END<<<<<<P<P<P<<<<<<<
```

BUTTON 3
```
>>>>>>>>>>>>>M
M<<<<<L<L<L<L<L<<<<<
>>>L>L>L>L>L>L>L>L>L>>>M
M<<D<D<L<X<L<L<L<X<L<D<D<<
>D>D>D>D>L>L>L>L>D>D>D>DM
D>D>D>G>D>B>L>L>B>D>G>D>D>M
MD<D<G<D<D<B<B<P<B<B<D<G<D<D
>D>G>D>D>B>B>P>B>B>D>D>G>D>M
M<D<D<G<D<B<P<B<P<B<D<G<D<<
>>D>D>D>B>B>B>B>B>D>D>D>>M
M<<D<D<B<B<B<B<B<B<D<D<<
>>>D>D>B>B>B>B>B>D>D>D>>>M
M<<<<D<B<B<B<B<B<D<<<<
>>>>>B>B>B>B>B>B>>>>>M
M<<<<<B<B<B<B<B<B<<<<<
>>>>>B>B>B>B>B>B>>>>>M
END<<<<<B<B<B<B<B<<<<<
```

BUTTON 4
```
>>>>>>G>G>G>G>G>>>>>>M
M<<<<<G<<<<<<G<<<<<
>>>>G>>>L>L>L>>>G>>>>M
M<B<<<G<<L<L<L<L<<G<<<<
B>B>B>>G>>L>X>L>X>L>>G>>>B>M
M<B<<<G<<L<X<L<X<L<<G<<B<B
>>>>G>>>L>L>L>>>G>>>B>M
M<<<<G<<<<L<<<<G<<<<
>>>>G>>>L>L>L>>>G>>>>M
M<G<G<G<G<G<G<G<G<G<G<G<G<G<G<
G>L>G>L>G>L>G>L>G>L>G>L>G>L>G>L>GM
MG<G<B<G<B<G<B<G<G<G<B<G<B<G<B<G<G
>G>G>G>G>G>G>G>Y>G>G>G>G>G>G>M
M<<<<<<Y<Y<Y<<<<<<<
>>>>>>Y>Y>Y>Y>Y>>>>>>M
M<<<<<Y<Y<R<Y<R<Y<Y<<<<
>>>>R>R>R>R>R>R>R>R>R>>>>END
```

PAGE 102-105 DECOMPOSITION

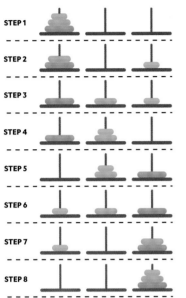

STEP 1

STEP 2

STEP 3

STEP 4

STEP 5

STEP 6

STEP 7

STEP 8

PAGE 108-109 SAVE THE SATELLITE

```
>>>>R>>>>D
D<<<<B<G<B<<<<
>>>G>Y>R>R>G>>>D
D<<<B<B<Y<B<Y<<<<
>>R>Y>R>G>G>B>G>>D
D<<G<R<B<B<R<Y<Y<<
>>B>B>>>>B>R>>D
D<<G<R<<<<Y<B<<
>>Y>R>>>>G>B>>D
D<<B<Y<<<<Y<R<<
>>Y>R>G>R>Y>R>G>>D
D<<B<R<Y<Y<B<G<B<<
>G>G>B>G>R>Y>B>R>G>D
D<B<Y<G<B<B<R<Y<B<R<
G>R>B>B>R>Y>Y>G>B>G>RD
DY<Y<G<R<<<<Y<R<G<B
R>B>Y>>>>>>R>YD
G>R>>>>>>>Y>BD
END<B<<<<<<<B<
```

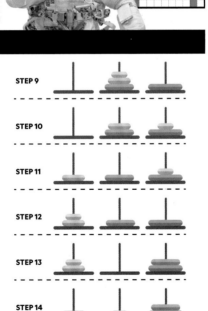

CHAPTER 4

PAGE 118-119 CODY'S BACKPACK

Our Solution:

Spare parts (.25 lb, .11 kg)

Rope (12 lb, 5.4 kg)

Camera battery (.13 lb, .05 kg)

Camera (.34 lb, .15 kg)

Total: 12.72 pounds (5.7 kg)

PAGE 122-123 MAKING SHAPES

DO REPEAT **3** TIMES
MOVE FORWARD 12 INCHES (31 CM)

MAKE A DOT ON THE GROUND

TURN RIGHT

DO REPEAT **3** TIMES
MOVE FORWARD 12 INCHES

MAKE A DOT ON THE GROUND

TURN RIGHT

DO REPEAT **3** TIMES
MOVE FORWARD 12 INCHES

MAKE A DOT ON THE GROUND

TURN RIGHT

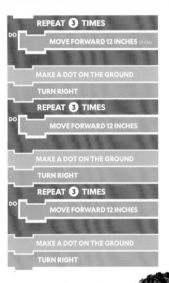

PAGE 124-125 SETTING UP THE PICTURE

Our Solution:

TOUCH MARKER TO THE GROUND

MOVE FORWARD 1 YARD (1 M)

TURN RIGHT

DO REPEAT **3** TIMES
MOVE FORWARD 1 YARD

TURN RIGHT

MOVE FORWARD 1 YARD

TURN RIGHT

DO REPEAT **3** TIMES
MOVE FORWARD 1 YARD

PAGE 106-107 MIRROR MOVING

STEP 1

STEP 2

STEP 3

STEP 4

STEP 5

STEP 6

STEP 7

STEP 8

STEP 9

STEP 10

STEP 11

STEP 12

STEP 13

STEP 14

STEP 15

STEP 16

Frog

IF THE UP ARROW IS CLICKED THEN
  DISPLAY THE PHOTO
ELSE
  WAIT 3 SECONDS AND DISPLAY THE NEXT PHOTO TO THE RIGHT

IF THE UP ARROW IS CLICKED THEN
  DISPLAY THE PHOTO
ELSE
  WAIT 3 SECONDS AND DISPLAY THE NEXT PHOTO TO THE RIGHT

IF THE UP ARROW IS CLICKED THEN
  DISPLAY THE PHOTO
ELSE
  WAIT 3 SECONDS AND DISPLAY THE NEXT PHOTO TO THE RIGHT

IF THE UP ARROW IS CLICKED THEN
  DISPLAY THE PHOTO
ELSE
  WAIT 3 SECONDS AND DISPLAY THE NEXT PHOTO TO THE RIGHT

IF THE UP ARROW IS CLICKED THEN
  DISPLAY THE PHOTO
ELSE
  WAIT 3 SECONDS AND DISPLAY THE NEXT PHOTO TO THE RIGHT

IF THE UP ARROW IS CLICKED THEN
  DISPLAY THE PHOTO
ELSE
  WAIT 3 SECONDS AND DISPLAY THE NEXT PHOTO TO THE RIGHT

Snake

IF THE UP ARROW IS CLICKED THEN
  DISPLAY THE PHOTO
ELSE
  WAIT 3 SECONDS AND DISPLAY THE NEXT PHOTO TO THE RIGHT

IF THE UP ARROW IS CLICKED THEN
  DISPLAY THE PHOTO
ELSE
  WAIT 3 SECONDS AND DISPLAY THE NEXT PHOTO TO THE RIGHT

IF THE UP ARROW IS CLICKED THEN
  DISPLAY THE PHOTO
ELSE
  WAIT 3 SECONDS AND DISPLAY THE NEXT PHOTO TO THE RIGHT

IF THE UP ARROW IS CLICKED THEN
  DISPLAY THE PHOTO
ELSE
  WAIT 3 SECONDS AND DISPLAY THE NEXT PHOTO TO THE RIGHT

IF THE UP ARROW IS CLICKED THEN
  DISPLAY THE PHOTO
ELSE
  WAIT 3 SECONDS AND DISPLAY THE NEXT PHOTO TO THE RIGHT

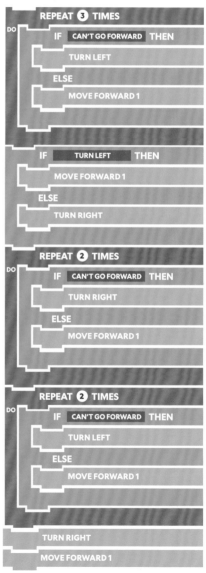

PAGE 134-135 GETTING HOME

Our Solution:

REPEAT 3 TIMES
DO
  IF CAN'T GO FORWARD THEN
    TURN LEFT
  ELSE
    MOVE FORWARD 1

IF TURN LEFT THEN
  MOVE FORWARD 1
ELSE
  TURN RIGHT

REPEAT 2 TIMES
DO
  IF CAN'T GO FORWARD THEN
    TURN RIGHT
  ELSE
    MOVE FORWARD 1

REPEAT 2 TIMES
DO
  IF CAN'T GO FORWARD THEN
    TURN LEFT
  ELSE
    MOVE FORWARD 1

TURN RIGHT

MOVE FORWARD 1

Our Solutions:

Blue path:

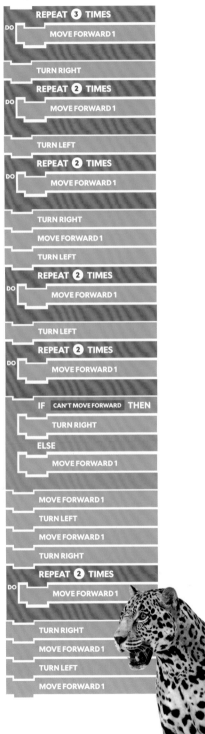

```
        REPEAT 3 TIMES
DO          MOVE FORWARD 1

        TURN RIGHT
        REPEAT 2 TIMES
DO          MOVE FORWARD 1

        TURN LEFT
        REPEAT 2 TIMES
DO          MOVE FORWARD 1

        TURN RIGHT
        MOVE FORWARD 1
        TURN LEFT
        REPEAT 2 TIMES
DO          MOVE FORWARD 1

        TURN LEFT
        REPEAT 2 TIMES
DO          MOVE FORWARD 1

        IF   CAN'T MOVE FORWARD   THEN
            TURN RIGHT
        ELSE
            MOVE FORWARD 1

        MOVE FORWARD 1
        TURN LEFT
        MOVE FORWARD 1
        TURN RIGHT
        REPEAT 2 TIMES
DO          MOVE FORWARD 1

        TURN RIGHT
        MOVE FORWARD 1
        TURN LEFT
        MOVE FORWARD 1
```

Orange path:

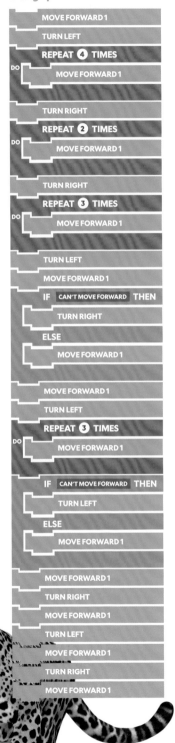

```
        MOVE FORWARD 1
        TURN LEFT
        REPEAT 4 TIMES
DO          MOVE FORWARD 1

        TURN RIGHT
        REPEAT 2 TIMES
DO          MOVE FORWARD 1

        TURN RIGHT
        REPEAT 3 TIMES
DO          MOVE FORWARD 1

        TURN LEFT
        MOVE FORWARD 1
        IF   CAN'T MOVE FORWARD   THEN
            TURN RIGHT
        ELSE
            MOVE FORWARD 1

        MOVE FORWARD 1
        TURN LEFT
        REPEAT 3 TIMES
DO          MOVE FORWARD 1

        IF   CAN'T MOVE FORWARD   THEN
            TURN LEFT
        ELSE
            MOVE FORWARD 1

        MOVE FORWARD 1
        TURN RIGHT
        MOVE FORWARD 1
        TURN LEFT
        MOVE FORWARD 1
        TURN RIGHT
        MOVE FORWARD 1
```

Green path:

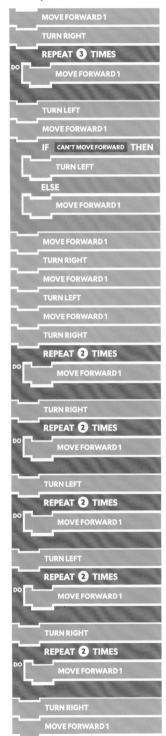

```
        MOVE FORWARD 1
        TURN RIGHT
        REPEAT 3 TIMES
DO          MOVE FORWARD 1

        TURN LEFT
        MOVE FORWARD 1
        IF   CAN'T MOVE FORWARD   THEN
            TURN LEFT
        ELSE
            MOVE FORWARD 1

        MOVE FORWARD 1
        TURN RIGHT
        MOVE FORWARD 1
        TURN LEFT
        MOVE FORWARD 1
        TURN RIGHT
        REPEAT 2 TIMES
DO          MOVE FORWARD 1

        TURN RIGHT
        REPEAT 2 TIMES
DO          MOVE FORWARD 1

        TURN LEFT
        REPEAT 2 TIMES
DO          MOVE FORWARD 1

        TURN LEFT
        REPEAT 2 TIMES
DO          MOVE FORWARD 1

        TURN RIGHT
        REPEAT 2 TIMES
DO          MOVE FORWARD 1

        TURN RIGHT
        MOVE FORWARD 1
```

GO FURTHER!

>> **READY TO TRY SOME MORE-ADVANCED PROGRAMMING?**
Apply what you know, and give these additional activities a try.

A BATTY BINARY SEARCH

Write a binary search tree for this crazy creature!

Rosy-lipped batfish live in the waters off Cocos Island, near Costa Rica. They use their fins to walk along the seafloor.

Here's a suggestion to start you out.

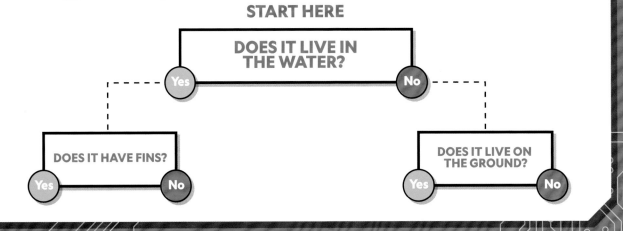

START HERE

DOES IT LIVE IN THE WATER?

Yes   No

DOES IT HAVE FINS?

Yes   No

DOES IT LIVE ON THE GROUND?

Yes   No

MAKE YOUR OWN BINARY CODE!

You can make your own binary code out of almost anything. Just choose two objects to represent the parts of your code. Then, write a message to someone else using your code, and ask them to read it!

YOUR HOME: THE MAZE

Hide a surprise in a room in your home. **Write an algorithm** to help a family member find the surprise by starting in a different room.

MORE TO TRY! >>

GO FURTHER

YOUR OWN LANGUAGE

Write your own cryptogram using symbols! First, write the alphabet on a piece of paper—then think of a different symbol to represent each letter. Draw the symbols under the alphabet. This is your key. Write a message to someone using the symbols. Give them a copy of the key, and ask them to decode the message. Be as creative with your symbols as you can—use different colors, shapes, and sizes!

IF/ELSE SIMON SAYS GAME

If ...

Grab some friends for some active fun by playing a **Code This type of Simon Says!**

In this version, it's the programmer's job to say commands—and the computers' job is to follow them!

For example, the programmer says, "IF I raise my right hand, you jump. ELSE you stand still." Any computer that doesn't follow the command correctly is out. How fast can the computers follow the programmer's commands?

OPTIMIZED SLIME

Make some super slime using the recipe to the left (first ask a parent for permission and help!). Then optimize your slime by adding some of the special ingredients. Write down how adding the special ingredients changes the slime. Which makes …

… the softest slime?

… the fluffiest slime?

… the squishiest slime?

WHAT TO DO

1   MIX THE GLUE AND SHAVING CREAM in a plastic container.

2   Stir in the **SALINE SOLUTION** a little at a time until the mixture stops being sticky.

CODE ON

BLOCK COMMANDS ARE A GREAT WAY TO START LEARNING TO CODE. But most programming is done by writing code in languages. Just like any language, programming languages like JavaScript, Python, and Ruby have words and specific orders to write them in.

THINK ABOUT IT

If you said "Today, hello, are? how you" no one would know what you meant. It's the same with computer programming—coders need to use the correct words in the correct order.

HTML/JAVASCRIPT

Here's some code in HTML/JavaScript. In this game, the computer picks a "right" answer number between 1 and 10 at random.

```
<!DOCTYPE html>
<html>
<body>

<p>I'm thinking of a number.  Can you guess it?
Type in a number between 1 and 10.</p>

<input id = "myInput" type = "text">

<button onclick = "myFunction()">Is it right?</button>

<p id = "demo"></p>

<script>
var correct = Math.floor(Math.random() * 10) + 1;
function myFunction() {
    var guessBox = document.getElementById("myInput");
    var guess = Number(guessBox.value);
    var text;

    // If the guess is correct
    if (correct === guess) {
       text = "That's it! Great job!";
    // If the guess is too high
    } else if (guess > correct) {
       text = "Try lower.";
    // If the guess is too low
    } else {
       text = "Try higher.";
    }
    document.getElementById("demo").innerHTML = text;
}
</script>

</body>
</html>
```

These "words" are part of the programming language. They tell the computer things like where this section of the webpage starts.

These are the actual words that someone playing the game will see on their screen. The code pair <p> </p> tells the computer where the paragraph of text starts and ends.

This command tells the button on the screen how to work.

This command sequence is the If/Else command. It tells the computer how to respond to the player's guess. If the player guesses the number the computer picked, the text on the computer will read, "That's it! Great job." If the player guesses a number too high, the text will read, "Try lower." And if the player guesses a number too low, the text will read, "Try higher."

I'm thinking of a number. Can you guess it? Type in a number between 1 and 10.

| 2 | | **Is it right?** |

Try higher.

PYTHON

Here's the game written in Python.

```python
import random
num = random.randint(1, 10)
while True:
    print("I'm thinking of a number.  Can you guess
    it?  Type in a number between 1 and 10")
    guess = input()
    i = int(guess)
    if i == num:
        print("Great job!")
        break
    elif i < num:
        print("Try Higher")
    elif i > num:
        print("Try Lower")
```

This code tells the computer to pick a "right" answer number between 1 and 10.

These are the actual words that someone playing the game will see on their screen. The code "print" tells the computer what text to display.

This command sequence is the If/Else command. It tells the computer how to respond to the player's guess. If the play guesses the number the computer picked, the text on the screen will read "Great job!" If the player guesses a number too low, the text on the screen will read "Try Higher." If the player guesses a number too high, the text on the screen will read "Try Lower."

TRY IT OUT

Now that you've mastered the ideas behind coding, it's time to put them to work. With an adult's permission, visit these sites for more in-depth coding practice.

CODE.ORG
code.org
Kid-friendly coding courses, plus additional resources

CODEACADEMY
codecademy.com
In-depth tutorials appropriate for older learners such as teens and adults

SCRATCH
scratch.mit.edu
Kid-friendly games, tutorials, and a free off-line editor

Code thisssssss!

GLOSSARY

algorithm: a set of steps or list of instructions a computer uses to accomplish a goal

ASCII: A type of binary code that represents letters, numbers, and symbols (ASCII stands for American Standard Code for Information)

binary: made of two things

binary code: code that uses two symbols to represent letters, numbers, and other characters

binary search: the process of repeatedly dividing a large amount of information into two to find a specific piece of information

bug: a mistake in computer code that causes a computer program to run poorly or in a way that is not expected

cipher: a message written in a secret language

cipher wheel: a tool used to write and decode ciphers

code: the specific directions written for a computer to follow

coding: the process of thinking about and writing down instructions for a computer

combine: to put two or more parts of something together

command: an instruction that a computer follows

computer science: the study of how to write logical computer programs

conditional: a piece of code that causes a computer to choose one of two paths

constraint: anything that might keep a solution to a problem from working (or working well)

cryptology: the study of writing and breaking codes

debugging: the process of going through code to find problems

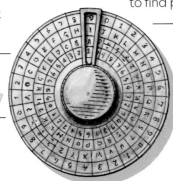

decomposition: the process of breaking down a problem into smaller parts that are easier to solve

efficient: working in the best possible way

event: anything that causes a computer program to run a certain way

global positioning system (GPS): a tool that uses computers and satellite signals to help people to find their location on Earth

graphics: the pictures that computers make by reading code

labyrinth: a maze

logic: thinking about something in a way that makes sense

loop: a set of steps that are followed over and over again

Lovelace, Ada: English countess who wrote the first algorithm and is considered to be the world's first computer programmer

Morse code: a type of binary code made of dots and dashes (short and long signals)

optimize: to write computer code so that it works best for a particular situation

pixel: a tiny piece of a picture on a computer screen

programming: the process of writing code for computers

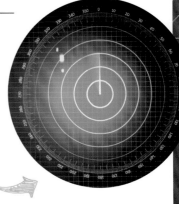

sonar: a tool that uses sound waves bouncing off of something to determine its location

strategy: a plan used to accomplish a goal

substitution cipher: a message written in a secret language in which each letter is replaced by a different symbol

Traveling Salesperson: a computer logic problem that asks the user to find the shortest path between a group of points

trial and error: a way to solve problems that involves making a guess, being wrong, and then guessing again

user: a person that uses a computer

INDEX

Illustrations are indicated by **boldface.**

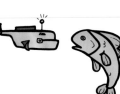

CREDITS

Any more bugs?

DR: Dreamstime; GI: Getty Images; SS: Shutterstock

Cover:

(3D animation on computer screen), Andia/UIG via GI; (smiling teen girl), valentinrussanov/E+/GI; (laptop computer), artjazz/SS; (go-Pro style camera), NaMaKuKi/SS; (multi-color binary code (for T-shirt), BEST-BACKGROUNDS/SS; (pixel owl), paramouse/SS; (green binary code texture), Valery Brozhinsky/SS; (paper plate), PARINKI/SS; (paper fastener), Andre Bonn/SS; Back cover, Lori Epstein/NGK Staff

Front matter:

1, Titima Ongkantong/SS; 2-3 (BACKGROUND), Valery Brozhinsky/SS; 2 (UP LE), chuckchee/SS; 2 (LO), GeorgeRudy/iStock/GI; 2 (crystal), Sebastian Janicki/SS; 2 (top spider), Zety Akhzar/SS; 2 (right spider), Sutthituch/SS; 2 (middle spider), fivespots/SS; 2 (left spider), Nyvlt-art/SS; 3 (cobra), William Robson/SS; 3 (moths), Mikhail Melnikov/SS; 3 (ruler), SmileStudio/SS; 3 (multicolored pens), Olga Popova/SS; 3 (white paper), Stephen Rees/SS; 4 (LE), Jason Edwards/National Geographic Creative; 4 (LO), melissaf84/SS; 5 (UP), NASA; 5 (RT), National Geographic Image Collection/Alamy; 5 (LO), Jagodka/SS; 6 (UP), Sandra van der Steen/SS; 6 (LE), ifong/SS; (dalmation), JStaley401; (dog), Dorottya Mathe/SS; (cat), Elena Rudyk/SS; (rabbit), djem/SS; (bird), Eric Isselee/SS; (lizard), Robert Eastman/SS; (fish), Mikael Damkier/SS; (hamster), Eric Isselee/SS; (frog), halimqd/SS; 6 (LO RT), Motovilova Yulia Dmitrievna/SS; 7 (UP LE), antoniodiaz/SS; 7 (UP RT), Mino Surkala/SS; 7 (CTR LE), NASA/JPL-Caltech/MSSS; 7 (LO LE), Andia/UIG/GI; 7 (RT), Robert Daly/GI; 8 (LO), aslysun/SS; 8 (CTR), Sladic/iStock/GI; 8 (RT), Sladic/iStock/GI; 9 (UP), ArcadeImages/Alamy; 9 (LO), timquo/SS; 10 (UP), Roger Meerts/SS; 10 (LO), Videowokart/SS; 12 (LO), Bradley Blackburn/SS; 12 (white flower), Minstrel25/SS; 13, Arunee Rodloy/SS; 14 (lily pads), Videowokart/SS; 15 (rock), Zodar/SS; 15 (white flower), Minstrel25/SS; 15 (frog), Rudmer Zwerver/SS; 15 (butterfly), Gary Stolz/USFWS; 15 (RT), Tonya Kay/SS; 15 (lily pads), Videowokart/SS; 16, Anna Omelchenko/SS; 17 (UP), MC_PP/SS; 17 (LO), Willyam Bradberry/SS

Chapter 1:

20-21, Jason Edwards/National Geographic Creative; 22 (LE), Science & Society Picture Library/GI; 22 (RT), Eduardo Rivero/SS; 23 (banana), Maks Narodenko/SS; 23 (mixed berries), Elena Elisseeva/SS; 23 (raspberries), Ingram; 23 (blueberries), Valentyn Volkov/SS; 23 (banana slices), Rodica Ciorba/SS; 23 (peach slices), Tim UR/SS; 23 (blender), Rae Alexander/SS; 24 (tape), Freer/SS; 24 (pillow), GalapagosPhoto/SS; 24 (UP RT), Gyuszko/DR; 24 (paper ball), Photodisc; 25 (clipboard and pencil), photastic/SS; 25 (UP LE), Lori Epstein/NGK Staff; 25 (UP RT), Lori Epstein/NGK Staff; 25 (LO), Lori Epstein/NGK Staff; 26-27 (BACKGROUND), romakoma/SS; 27, Joaquin Ossorio Castillo/SS; 28, Ratthaphong Ekariyasap/SS; 29 (UP), studioVin/SS; 29 (LO), Julian Rovagnati/SS; 29 (RT), Valery Kraynov/SS; 30, U.S. Geological Survey/photo by Vivian R. Queija; 31, Petr Bonek/SS; 32, Everett Collection Inc/Alamy; 33 (alphabet letters a, b, d, e, g, h, k, l, n, s, t, v, w, x, y), Tupungato/SS; 33 (alphabet letters c, f, i, j, m, o, p, q, r, u, z), Eyethink Pictures/SS; 33 (BACKGROUND), Thinkstock; 34 (LE), Matthew Orselli/SS; 34 (RT), sekundemal/SS; 35 (UP LE), Mirek Kijewski/SS; 35 (UP RT), Andrea Izzotti/SS; 35 (CTR LE), Volt Collection/SS; 35 (LO LE), Dirk Ercken/DR; 35 (LO RT), Sarah Cheriton-Jo/SS; 36 (UP), Rungsuriya Chareesri/SS; 36 (UP RT), Ingram; 36 (pencil), Christophe Testi/DR; 36 (paper fastener), Andre Bonn/SS; 36 (paper plate), PARINKI/SS; 37 (UP), Lori Epstein/NGK Staff; 37 (LO), Lori Epstein/NGK Staff; 37 (INSET), Lori Epstein/NGK Staff; 38 (UP), Lori Epstein/NGK Staff; 38 (LO), Lori Epstein/NGK Staff; 38 (paper plate), PARINKI/SS; 39 (UP RT), Lori Epstein/NGK Staff; 39 (LO), Butterfly Hunter/SS; 39 (paper plate), PARINKI/SS; 40-41, Samantha Reinders/National Geographic Society; 41, Traktirman/SS; 42, Eric Isselee/SS; 42-43, kchungtw/iStock/GI; 44 (tape), Freer/SS; 44 (chalk), Mr Doomits/SS; 44 (LO), Paulus Rusyanto/DR; 45 (LO), Eric Isselee/SS; 45 (UP), Hue Ta/SS; 46, Suwat Sirivutcharungchit/SS; 47 (leaves), MichaelJay/iStockphoto; 47 (mushrooms), Valentina Razumova/SS; 48-49, Light & Magic Photography/DR; 48, Henrik Larsson/SS; 49 (UP LE), Zety Akhzar/SS; 49 (UP RT), Sutthituch/SS; 49 (CTR), fivespots/SS; 49 (LO LE), Nyvlt-art/SS; 49 (LO RT), Sebastian Janicki/SS; 50-51, Jason Edwards/National Geographic Creative; 51 (red mask), Adisa/SS; 51 (vase), Rogers Fund, 1907/Metropolitan Museum of Art; 51 (green mask), Bequest of Jane Costello Goldberg, from the Collection of Arnold I. Goldberg, 1986/Metropolitan Museum of Art; 51 (gold bowl), The Cesnola Collection, Purchased by subscription, 1874-76/Metropolitan Museum of Art; 51 (crown), aquariagirl1970/SS; 51 (old books), Zhukov Oleg/SS; 51 (helmet), Andrew Bzh/SS; 51 (goblet), Gift of J. Pierpont Morgan, 1917/Metropolitan Museum of Art; 51 (jug), Gift of the Greek Government, 1930/Metropolitan Museum of Art; 51 (LO), Kb7rut/DR

Chapter 2:

54-55, melissaf84/SS; 56-57 (BACKGROUND), 2009fotofriends/SS; 56-57 (rocks), AlexussK/SS; 56 (LE), Valt Ahyppo/SS; 56 (CTR), BristolK/Alamy; 56 (RT), M.M.art/SS; 57 (LE), Butterfly Hunter/SS; 57 (CTR), Marijus Auruskevicius/SS; 57 (RT), LFRabanedo/SS; 58-59 (red blocks), Vadym Lavra/SS; 58-59 (coins), Anthony Pleva/Alamy; 58 (LO RT), FloridaStock/SS; 58 (LO LE), Image provided courtesy of University of Calgary Archives 84.005_63.30; 60-61 (BACKGROUND), Arctic Images/Alamy; 60-61 (basket), Mike Flippo/SS; 60-61 (dog and cat), Jagodka/SS; 60 (LO RT), Alexey Seafarer/SS; 62 (BACKGROUND), fotomak/SS; 62 (LO), Eric Isselee/SS; 63 (frog), Antonio Guillem Fernández/Alamy; 63 (ruler), SmileStudio/SS; 63 (rock), AlexussK/SS; 63 (pencil), Christophe Testi/DR; 64-65 (cups), Elnur/DR; 64-65 (pen), Petlyaroman/DR; 64 (moths), Mikhail Melnikov/SS; 64 (Edison), Everett Historical/SS; 64 (paper), pockygallery/SS; 66 (LO), chuckchee/SS; 66-67 (cups), Elnur/DR; 68 (CTR), Art tools design/SS; 68 (LO), Independent birds/SS; 69 (LO), Open Government Licence/Alamy; 69 (UP), Rich Reid/National Geographic Creative; 70 (flashlight), Alexander Pladdet/DR; 70 (bike), Vladyslav Starozhylov/SS; 71 (flashlight), Alexander Pladdet/DR; 71 (pencil), Tharakorn Arunothai/SS; 71 (LO), Science Museum/SSPL/GI/GI; 72, Eric Isselee/SS; 73, Galushko Sergey/SS; 75, MZPHOTO.CZ/SS; 76, Ondrej Prosicky/SS; 77, Anton Rodionov/SS; 78, Dean Drobot/SS; 79 (bird in tree), steve52/SS; 79 (raccoon in tree), Heiko Kiera/SS; 79 (tree), Zerbor/SS; 79 (LO LE), Stevebyland/DR; 79 (LO CTR), Sonsedska Yuliia/SS; 80-81 (BACKGROUND), AF archive/Alamy; 80-81 (angler fish), Solvin Zankl/Alamy; 80-81 (vampire squid), Steve Downer/Science Source; 80-81 (spider crab), f11photo/SS; 80-81 (tubeworm), SeaPics.com; 81, Teeraparp Maythavee/DR

Chapter 3:

84-85, NASA; 86, Rich Carey/SS; 88 (LE), Hugo Felix/SS; 88-89 (keyboard), rangizzz/SS; 89, matthew25/SS; 90 (LE), chuckchee/SS; 90-91 (green balloon), Comaniciu Dan/SS; 90 (LO RT), photographyfirm/SS; 91 (UP), M_T/SS; 91 (tape), Flas100/SS; 91 (RT), Lori Epstein/NGK Staff; 92 (RT), Lori Epstein/NGK Staff; 92 (LO), Djem82/DR; 92 (LE), Comaniciu Dan/SS; 93 (UP), Lori Epstein/NGK Staff; 93 (LO), Courtesy Brookhaven National Laboratory; 94-95, NASA/SS; 95 (UP), Grigorita Ko/SS; 95 (BACKGROUND), NASA; 96, ESB Professional/SS; 98 (graph paper), GreenBelka/SS; 98 (multicolored pens), Olga Popova/SS; 98 (LO), Kuttelvaserova Stuchelova/SS; 99, William Robson/SS; 101, William Robson/SS; 102 (UP), MNI/SS; 102 (LO), Alena Ozerova/SS; 103 (LE), Lori Epstein/NGK Staff; 103 (RT), Lori Epstein/NGK Staff; 104 (UP LE), Viorel Sima/SS; 104 (UP RT), Lori Epstein/NGK Staff; 104 (LO), Lori Epstein/NGK Staff; 105 (UP), Lori Epstein/NGK Staff; 105 (LO), Lori Epstein/NGK Staff; 106-107, Frank Whitney/GI; 106-107 (BACKGROUND), Tjefferson/SS; 108-109, NASA/Jim Grossmann; 109, Castleski/SS

Chapter 4:

112-115, National Geographic Image Collection/Alamy; 114 (mask and snorkel), Kletr/SS; 114 (swimsuit), bonetta/iStockphoto; 114 (sunglasses), studiovin/SS; 114 (boots), Tony_C/SS; 114 (mittens), Vincent Giordano/DR; 114 (suitcase), Zynatis/SS; 114 (books), Prokrida/SS; 114 (umbrella), Evikka/SS; 114 (croquet balls), Bill Fehr/SS; 115 (apple), Tim UR/SS; 115 (wooden sticks), Luciano Cosmo/SS; 115 (aluminum foil), Picsfive/SS; 115 (pencil and paper), Vitaly Korovin/DR; 116 (tape), Fotoschab/DR; 116 (potato), STILLFX/SS; 116 (plastic bag), snyferok/iStockphoto; 116 (UP RT), Lori Epstein/NGK Staff; 116 (LO), Lori Epstein/NGK Staff; 117, Lori Epstein/NGK Staff; 118 (UP RT), skodonnell/iStock/GI; 118 (candy), Nigel Monckton/DR; 118 (battery), Jamesboy Nuchaikong/SS; 118 (sunscreen), Bet_Noire/iStock/GI; 118 (LO RT), Kevin Xu Photography/SS; 118 (LO LE), skodonnell/GI; 118 (CTR LE), marekusz/SS; 119 (UP LE), wragg/iStock/GI; 119 (UP CTR), Infinitum Produx/SS; 119 (UP RT), Smit/SS; 119 (CTR RT), Lizard/SS; 119 (books), Anthony Shaw/DR; 119 (LO LE), wragg/iStock/GI; 119 (LO RT), Tatiana Ermakova/DR; 119 (frame), hxdbzxy/SS; 120, Eric Isselee/SS; 121 (blue pencil), Pan Stock/SS; 121 (blank paper), tomograf/iStock/GI; 122 (UP), Nino-Sayompoo/SS; 122 (LO), Kellen Slight/SS; 122 (chalk), Mr Doomits/SS; 123 (UP), Lori Epstein/NGK Staff; 123 (LO), The Asahi Shimbun/GI; 124-127, PhotocechCZ/SS; 126 (UP), GCShutter/iStock/GI; 126 (LO), Rudmer Zwerver/SS; 127 (bison), Steve Degenhardt/DR; 127 (frog), Dirk Ercken/DR; 127 (snake), Matt Jeppson/SS; 127 (penguins), Bernard Breton/DR; 127 (tiger), Akbar Solo/DR; 127 (spider), Arno van Dulmen/SS; 127 (turtle), Charles Brutlag/SS; 127 (polar bears), Tom linster/SS; 127 (tropical fish), KKulikov/SS; 128-131, evenfh/SS; 128, cynoclub/SS; 129 (CTR), My Life Graphic/SS; 129 (LO), Piccaya/DR; 130 (UP), photastic/SS; 130 (coins), Asaf Eliason/SS; 130 (LO), GeorgeRudy/iStock/GI; 131 (UP), Eric Isselee/SS; 131 (LO), Edwin Butter/SS; 132-135 (grass bundles), Anton-Burakov/SS; 132 (rocks), My Life Graphic/SS; 132-135 (butterflies), Anna Bakulina/DR; 132-135 (flowers), Brand X; 132 (jaguar), zemkooo/SS; 132-135 (CTR), PhotoJoJay/SS; 133 (rocks), My Life Graphic/SS; 134 (RT), one photo/SS; 134 (LO), Eric Isselee/SS; 135 (rocks), My Life Graphic/SS; 136 (rocks), My Life Graphic/SS; 136-139 (BACKGROUND), elioemg/SS; 136 (LO), Anan Kaewkhammul/SS; 137 (rocks), My Life Graphic/SS; 138-141, Stocktrek Images, Inc./Alamy; 139 (UP LE), Seth Wenig/AP/SS; 139 (UP RT), Dan Rowley/SS; 139 (CTR RT), The Art Archive/SS; 139 (LO RT), Elise Amendola/AP/SS

End Matter:

140 (UP RT), Volt Collection/SS; 140 (UP LE), bergamont/SS; 140 (raspberries), Ingram; 140 (blueberries), Valentyn Volkov/SS; 140 (banana slices), Rodica Ciorba/SS; 140 (peach slices), Tim UR/SS; 140 (blender), Rae Alexander/SS; 140 (CTR), Petr Bonek/SS; 140 (letter A), Tupungato/SS; 140 (letter Z), Eyethink Pictures/SS; 140 (LO CTR), Matthew Orselli/SS; 140 (LO LE), Julian Rovagnati/SS; 141 (UP LE), Eric Isselee/SS; 141 (leaves), MichaelJay/iStockphoto; 141 (mushrooms), Valentina Razumova/SS; 141 (UP RT), Henrik Larsson/SS; 141 (crystal), Sebastian Janicki/SS; 141 (LO LE), Andrew Bzh/SS; 141 (red mask), Adisa/SS; 141 (jug), Gift of the Greek Government, 1930/Metropolitan Museum of Art; 141 (green mask), Bequest of Jane Costello Goldberg, from the Collection of Arnold I. Goldberg, 1986/Metropolitan Museum of Art; 141 (goblet), Gift of J. Pierpont Morgan, 1917/Metropolitan Museum of Art; 141 (crown), aquariagirl1970/SS; 141 (sea lion), Kb7rut/DR; 142 (UP LE), Valt Ahyppo/SS; 142 (UP RT), Eric Isselee/SS; 142 (CTR RT), Ondrej Prosicky/SS; 142 (LO), Jagodka/SS; 143 (angler fish), Solvin Zankl/Alamy; 143 (vampire squid), Steve Downer/Science Source; 143 (spider crab), f11photo/SS; 143 (tubeworm), SeaPics.com; 143 (UP RT), Rich Carey/SS; 143 (LO RT), Hugo Felix/SS; 144 (pixel animals), William Robson/SS; 144 (LE), ESB Professional/SS; 145 (UP LE), Alena Ozerova/SS; 145 (CTR), Castleski/SS; 145 (UP RT), skodonnell/iStock/GI; 145 (RT), PhotocechCZ/SS; 146 (UP), Dirk Ercken/DR; 146 (LO LE), Matt Jeppson/SS; 146 (rocks), My Life Graphic/SS; 147, Anan Kaewkhammul/SS; 148, WaterFrame/Alamy Stock Photo; 149 (paper and pencil), Amared Metawisai/SS; 149 (green apple), Maks Narodenko/SS; 149 (red apple), Dionisvera/SS; 149 (pennies), Asaf Eliason/SS; 149 (LO), Mike Flippo/SS; 150 (paper texture) Stephen Rees/Shutterstock; 150, kurhan/SS; 151 (cream), Love the wind/SS; 151 (slime), jarabee123/SS; 151 (glue), Mega Pixel/SS; 151 (saline solution), kenary820/SS; 153, Eric Isselee/SS; 154 (LE), winui/SS; 154 (RT), Dorling Kindersley/GI; 155 (LE), cigdem/SS; 155 (RT), MyImages - Micha/SS; 155 (LO), Science & Society Picture Library/GI; 159, Roger Meerts/SS

Since 1888, the National Geographic Society has funded more than 12,000 research, exploration, and preservation projects around the world. The Society receives funds from National Geographic Partners, LLC, funded in part by your purchase. A portion of the proceeds from this book supports this vital work. To learn more, visit **natgeo.com/info.**

For more information, visit nationalgeographic.com, call 1-800-647-5463, or write to the following address:

National Geographic Partners
1145 17th Street N.W.
Washington, D.C. 20036-4688 U.S.A.

Visit us online at **nationalgeographic.com/books**

For librarians and teachers:
ngchildrensbooks.org

More for kids from National Geographic:
natgeokids.com

National Geographic Kids magazine inspires children to explore their world with fun yet educational articles on animals, science, nature, and more. Using fresh storytelling and amazing photography, *Nat Geo Kids* shows kids ages 6 to 14 the fascinating truth about the world—and why they should care. **kids.nationalgeographic.com/subscribe**

For information about special discounts for bulk purchases, please contact National Geographic Books Special Sales: **specialsales@natgeo.com**

For rights or permissions inquiries, please contact National Geographic Books Subsidiary Rights: **bookrights@natgeo.com**

To Mike. Thanks for taking the journey with me. Thanks to Carlos Bueno for helping me to get started in the world of coding. The authors and publisher also wish to thank the book team: Shelby Lees, senior editor; Kathryn Williams, associate editor and illustrator; Lori Epstein, photo director; Danny Meldung, photo editor; Callie Broaddus, senior designer; Amanda Larsen, design director; Anne LeongSon and Gus Tello, production designers; Emma and Rory for participating in the photo shoot; Dr. Kyle Burke, associate professor of Computer Science and Technology, Plymouth State University; and Suzanne Sarraf and Tom Walton for their expertise in reviewing the code. —JS

Design by Fan Works Design

Library of Congress Cataloging-in-Publication Data

Names: Szymanski, Jennifer, author.
Title: Code this! / by Jennifer Szymanski.
Description: Washington, DC : National Geographic Kids, [2019] I Includes index. I Audience: Ages 9-12. I Audience: Grade 4 to 6.
Identifiers: LCCN 2018031628I ISBN 9781426334436 (pbk.) I ISBN 9781426334443 (hardcover)
Subjects: LCSH: Computer programming--Juvenile literature.
Classification: LCC QA76.6115 .S96 2019 I DDC 005.1--dc23
LC record available at https://lccn.loc.gov/2018031628

Printed in China
19/RRDS/1